WHY DOES YOUR DOG DO THAT?

GÖRAN BERGMAN

Why does your dog do that?

1977 - Fifth Printing

Howell Book House Inc.
New York

Published 1971 by HOWELL BOOK HOUSE INC.
730 Fifth Avenue, New York, New York 10019

Varför Gör Hunden Så?
© Göran Bergman 1967

Why Does Your Dog Do That?
English translation and line drawings
© Popular Dogs Publishing Co. Ltd. 1970

Library of Congress Catalog Card No. 73–165560
Printed in U.S.A.   ISBN 0-87605-808-X

CONTENTS

ILLUSTRATIONS

AUTHOR'S NOTE

I have written this book with the intention of awakening thought
in numerous matters concerning the behaviour of dogs which would
be of interest to many people and essential to every dog-owner.
Despite the enormous interest taken in dogs, hitherto there has
been no book giving an easily comprehensible outline of the
behaviour of dogs and the factors which determine the handling
of them in different situations. This book is based on modern
ethological research to the extent that it answers questions on
the special ethological characteristics of dogs, but is not scientific
in the sense that it is based on new investigations. Many views
and interpretations are based on my own experiences, and the
majority of the many examples that illustrate the text stem from
my own dogs.

Helsinki

INTRODUCTION

Get to know dogs in general and your own dog in particular! If you know what your dog does in different situations, why it does it and what it is expressing through different kinds of behaviour, then you are getting full value from your dog. If you are well informed on the behaviour of your dog and its mental requirements, then you avoid many mistakes in the training of it, whether it is just a pet, or a sporting dog or a dog used for some other purpose. Much of the contents of this book deals with the actual bringing up of dogs of different kinds, though it is not a textbook on the training of dogs. The aim of the book is to give the reader some idea of an ethologist's view of the dog as a biological phenomenon from an animal behaviour viewpoint, and as man's best friend in the animal world.

Today very few dogs are working dogs in the proper meaning of the word, but the pleasures of owning a dog are not dependent on a dog's usefulness. For the sportsman a dog is an invaluable companion in the largely instinctive behaviour patterns concerned with hunting and food-gathering. These in their turn are a fairly strongly sexually linked heritage from a past epoch in the development of man. But the sportsman usually also has quite different, purely emotional relations with his dog, and domestic dogs are perhaps sometimes substitutes for the outlet of maternal feelings. They may be simply for companionship, or a status symbol, whims of fashion or expressions of vanity. Breeding has many main-springs. The dog is the only one of our domestic animals which can fulfil so many diverse demands.

Wolves, the dog's ancestors, are adapted to a way of life in which both group life and solitary life, as well as family ties, play a large part. This diversity in way of life presupposes very full and expressive behaviour patterns and a highly developed ability to combine the elements of hereditary behaviour in different ways. The domestication of the wolf occurred at least twelve thousand years ago, and most of the many breeds of dogs which have gradually arisen differ outwardly from their wolf forbears very widely. Despite this, in dogs you find most perhaps even all the behaviour patterns found in wild wolves and which are decisive to their internal relations and way of life. The dog, on the other hand, has not developed anything new when it comes to instinctive actions. Perhaps one might venture to say that the dog, in its relatively secure domestic existence, has not had the chance to develop eventual genetically conditioned changes in basic behaviour patterns. Anyhow, it is clear that dogs show how constant basic hereditary behaviour patterns also remain under wholly different circumstances. The external characteristics of a dog and its disposition to carry out certain actions, on the other hand, vary very widely. Man has seen to it that both physical and emotional characteristics have acquired an extremely powerful artificial selection value—in the form of a more or less conscious selection in breeding. This is why the dog has developed in so many different directions. There is even a breed of dog, the Basenji, that does not bark, not to mention the very varied hunting behaviour and markedly different temperaments which different breeds show. Certain behaviour—or at least the disposition to carry out certain actions—in some cases deliberately, in others accidentally, has thus to a certain extent been eliminated in the choice that has led to the rise of different breeds.

But what is left of wolf behaviour in the dog is very significant—it is just this that makes 'the dog a dog'. And the reason why the wolf has been domesticated is that the wolf is to a certain extent a social animal. The cat—a solitary—is without doubt more or less equally highly developed as the dog and the wolf when it comes to behaviour that borders on intelligence. But despite centuries of domestication, the cat is still an animal which in its relationships with man does not show much social dependence. It is also illuminating that the lion, which for a feline animal shows an unusually clear tendency to group and domestic life, under skilled direction can more easily attain intimate relations with man than domestic cats in general show, after thousands of years of taming. Perhaps some non-dog-owners see the similarity between the behaviour of the wolf and the dog as something alarming and repellent, but what is ethologically wolf-like in a dog is in fact the prerequisite for a dog to be just as we would prefer it to be.

G.B.

1 SENSES

Dogs have the same kind of senses as human beings. But despite this a dog lives in a world of senses which is very differently constituted from our own. If we don't know what a dog's senses are registering, then we can have no clear idea of the reason for its behaviour. A dog's method of expression—its vocalisations, its facial expression, the position of its ears, its posture, and its movements—tells us a great deal about which sense in each separate situation is dominating the dog's behaviour. But without a fairly thorough knowledge of the sensitivity of the various senses, it is very easy to become a victim of misinterpretations. It is, in fact, not always easy to determine whether it is the sense of smell, vision or hearing which gives a dog the determining information in certain situations. Thus it has happened that a dog has gone blind without its owner noticing; a dog can find his way about in a familiar environment that well without the help of vision. But all dog-owners know that a dog in a town flat, for instance, as soon as it hears something alarming, runs to the window or some other position from where it can overlook the situation. Generally speaking, then, sight plays a very important rôle in a dog.

Investigations into the keenness and function of the senses in dogs are not easy to carry out, so over the years different researchers have come to rather different conclusions. Modern physiological research has given us the opportunity to eliminate a number, though perhaps not all, of erroneous sources in investigations into the senses of higher animals.

SENSE OF SMELL

Sensations of smell are extremely important to all dogs, not excepting even the most domesticated lap-dog. It can be said that we human beings are not capable of imagining the rich world of scent dogs live in. The olfactory membranes of a dog take up a one to ten thousand times larger area than those in man. The olfactory lobes, the parts of the brain which receive the olfactory nerve messages, are also very highly developed. An important circumstance is that a dog not only has a very sensitive sense of smell, but also has a well-developed ability to remember smells and relate this memory to different events, and with events the dog itself happens to have been involved in. There is a great deal of striking evidence to show how for years, sometimes for the whole of its life, a dog can remember scents which in some way or other have been related to some experience abhorrent to it, and naturally a dog also remembers those smells which are in some way related to pleasant events. My Scottish terrier, at a year old, was on a visit to a farm, when it came to grips with the farm's large powerful pointer. Seven years later the Scottie was sailing with me in the same area, and when the wind, at a distance of two kilometres from the farm, brought with it scents from the island on which the farm stood (the farm itself was not visible), the Scottie leapt agitatedly up on to the forepeak and then stayed there, growling and barking until we landed. The Scottie, who was generally not aggressive, took a great leap on to the jetty and like lightning attacked the farm's new and very friendly dog, which only in colour and size was similar to the antagonist from the Scottie's youth. The association between the scents of the area and the fight the Scottie had been involved in as a youngster was still, even after seven years, so strong that it totally dominated the Scottie's behaviour.

A dog's sense of smell is much more analytical than that of a

human being. Impressions of scent in a dog are probably constituted to give the dog the opportunity to differentiate between a
very large number of scents at the same time. Such a 'scent-picture'
of its environment cannot, of course, give information on shape and
distance, but is nevertheless something quite different from the
information our own sense of smell gives us. We can learn, for
instance, that two scents together give a certain sensation of smell,

With nostrils flared and head raised, the dog analyses an
interesting scent carried on the wind. If the scent is very weak,
the dog may close its eyes almost completely at the same time.

but without this previous experience it is mostly impossible for us
to know which components the smell is made up of. A dog's ability
to follow tracks or hunt out objects shows that dogs, in contrast to
human beings, really do separate very low scent intensities if
background scents of another kind are strong. A human's sense of
smell is highly sensitive only to a few scents—for instance the
by-products in smoke from cellulose-sulphate factories can be
sensed a hundred and fifty kilometres away from the factory. A
dog's nose is perhaps in a corresponding way sensitive to a large

B

number of scents, but considerably more important is its ability to differentiate between different scents.

Mixed sensations of scent are naturally also significant to dogs, for instance in situations such as when the dog is finding its way home from a place it has not been to before. A dog in a car is often following the route with the surrounding scents, without it necessarily showing in its behaviour. But a diversion from a route known to the dog is very obviously noticed as soon as the draught brings with it scents from surroundings which the dog does not know from previous journeys. On the deck of a boat, a dog notices scents from land to windward. I have seen my dachshund react strongly to such scents from a coast two kilometres to windward when our summer island on the leeward side is being passed. So the dog recognised the scents which the wind usually brings with it to the island, even in a situation in which it could neither see nor smell the island itself. It is relevant, of course, that our summer island is the dog's favourite place, a wonderful hunting-ground for field-mice and voles.

A number of sporting dogs appear to stick primarily to the scent of game in the air. They sniff upwards and note the scents which the wind brings with it from the tracks in which the game has moved. Other dogs follow more in detail the scents of the tracks themselves. Especially in the latter case, the scents can be presumed to consist of many other things apart from just the game's own scent. The ground and the vegetation in the tracks probably give off a great deal of scent which differs from those the ground gives off in other places. Many sporting dogs' ability to decide from tracks the direction in which, for instance, a hare has run, is quite simply astonishing. Presumably the dog is able after very little tracking, perhaps only a few yards, to decide in which direction the scent becomes stronger. Completely inexperienced dogs of breeds which track game are also skilled at this, but experience improves their skill.

Breeds with long noses and large nose volume all probably have a good sense of smell, while dogs with short noses or noses which are very pointed and have pinched nostrils can be presumed to have a somewhat less good sense of smell. When a dog sniffs the air, it draws in air in short gasps, dilates its nostrils, and at the same time often raises both its neck and head. Sometimes it also moves its nose from side to side. After a series of sniffing, short, indrawn breaths, it then breathes out with a short little sighing sound. If a dog closes its eyes slightly when sniffing, this means that it is experiencing a scent of something usually denoting pleasure, which it cannot immediately localise. One gets the impression that the dog is then excluding his sense of sight and hearing, and is concentrating solely on deciding on the direction of the source of the scent with the help of its nose. In many cases, however, the stimulation of the dog's olfactory sense will also stimulate its sight and hearing.

A dog's nose reacts strongly to certain scents in greater concentration. Alcohol fumes, for instance on a human being's breath, cause very light intensive sneezing; strong tobacco smoke has the same effect. A light blow on the nose, on the other hand, gives rise to sneeze reflexes which have nothing to do with scents. Dogs do not get ordinary colds. A number of terriers sneeze when they are led along tracks, perhaps because they then suddenly begin to scent strongly, which may irritate the scent membranes.

In daily life, however, despite its excellent sharp nose, a dog does not constantly analyse the scents around it in any marked way. Domestic dogs at home can be in a room for a long time or walk from room to room without showing any sign whatsoever of analysing the scents in its surroundings. But when a dog is not especially adjusted, it is also very sensitive to the analysis of every new scent. It notices, for instance, within a minute or so if anyone has brought in a piece of meat or something else it likes. A sleeping dog is naturally not so sensitive to scents as one which is awake. But it is, however, not at all difficult to waken a dog which is sound asleep with an olfactory sensation, but its reaction is seldom immediate. For instance, my dachshund can sleep on for quite a while with a piece of cheese in front of its nose before suddenly reacting.

Naturally the length of the delay depends on the strength of the stimulus and the dog's interest in the scent involved.

As in humans, a dog's sense of smell adapts itself to a certain stimulus level, and deviations and new scents are the first to be noted. Years of experience of dogs' reactions to different kinds of food at home show this very clearly.

SENSE OF VISION

A dog's sight is quite sharp and its ability to observe great. In practice, it can often be difficult to show that a dog does not see as well as a human being. In certain cases, a dog's lack of reaction may in fact be due more to the weaker 'intellectual capacity' of a dog's brain than to any possible optical defects or to the construction of the retina. Even such objects as a running field-mouse at fifty yards' distance on a shore, or a squirrel at a hundred yards' distance on the snow, can in a dog, which from experience knows that this little dot might be something interesting, cause the clearest reaction. But if the same dog happens to see the same object at the same distance in a place where the animal in question is perhaps not usually found, it can happen quite easily that there is no reaction at all. It can also happen that the dog does not understand what it sees, not that it is not able to see. But naturally these examples also show that the dog does not see enough detail to recognise an interesting object if it appears in an unexpected place some distance away from it.

Different dogs have very varying ability to recognise things in situations of this type. It is not by any means certain that these variations have anything to do with strength of vision. Often the temperament and curiosity of the dog play a large part. Most dogs can recognise people at distances varying between thirty and a hundred yards. At the latter distance, however, clothing seems to give the dog some help. My dachshunds can follow a flying gull with their eyes even if the gull moves two hundred yards away from them and at about a hundred yards they can easily distinguish between a crow and a gull—this is due to the fact that I feed the gulls at our summer cottage, but on the other hand usually drive away the crows, so the dachshunds naturally have learnt that crows are not welcome. In ordinary rooms, the dogs see flies sitting on the ceiling quite easily, but also often think that other dots are also flies. Broadly speaking, one can say that a dog sees roughly as well as a moderately short-sighted person without glasses.

A dog follows moving objects with its eyes and also judges distances quite well. It can, for instance, catch a ball and jump with precision. But it cannot compete with a cat, which is partly due to the fact that the cat, in relation to general anatomical build, represents greater specialisation for swift exact movements. Dogs have apparently no sense of vertigo, but at the same time they are afraid of falling or of being accidentally pushed down a slope or out of an open window.

The dog, like all mammals except the primates, lacks a fovea, a small area of the retina in which the sight cells, light-sensitive nerve cells, lie very close together and are not covered by blood-vessels. This explains why a dog cannot distinguish so many details as a human can. Normally a dog's retina has a well-developed tapetum, the reflecting area of the retinal side of the choroid. This reflected light then also influences the sight cells to some extent, thus making the picture more vivid. The tapetum is limited to the centre of the retina and the lower part of the field of vision; that is, the parts of the retina which normally receive a weak, but for the animal, essential picture. Dogs with weak general pigmentation have little pigment in the retina either. Their eyes do not reflect so much light and the reflected light is reddish, whilst dogs with rich pigmentation have eyes which usually shine green in the dark. The principle of reflection of light is the same as in traffic cat's-eyes. The lens and vitreous body break down the incoming light at the point on the retina and the tapetum in the retina then reflects some of the light, at which it is again broken down, and when leaving the eye is directed back towards the source of light. The often wide and almost circular pupil of a dog's eye means that one can see the details of the back of the eye quite easily in a weak light.

In the dark, a dog can see somewhat better than a human being, but that its vision is not especially good in weak light is shown in that dogs are unwilling to walk up steep stairs in the dark. But dachshunds anyhow can move surprisingly easily and swiftly, even in unknown territory, on the cloudiest of autumn evenings. A sense of smell and hearing obviously gives these short-legged dogs information on details of the ground so that they can move about almost as easily as in broad daylight.

When a dog is asleep, its eyes are positioned so that almost only the whites show and if you lift the upper lid the nictitating membrane covers more than half the front of the eye. Changes in the depth of the dog's sleep are reflected in the nictitating membrane's movements.

It has long been maintained that dogs are colour-blind. Recent very thorough research, however, into Cocker spaniels showed that it is possible to train dogs always to choose a bowl of a certain colour from a series of different coloured food-bowls. The degree of darkness and possible differences in scent, as well as the trainer's presence, could be eliminated as the reason why the dogs were able to distinguish between the different bowls. Naturally these experiments cannot prove that all breeds of dogs have the capacity to distinguish between colours, but it means that it is likely that most dogs can see colours, even if in general they are not aware of the significance of the object's colour. This is quite natural. A wolf's prey is generally mammals (which do not develop bright colours, but protective colouring), and its hunting habits are largely dependent on its sense of smell. In addition, the eye of a mammal is usually colour-blind in weak light and the wolf is a quite highly developed dusk-animal. Under these circumstances, the colour of an object is of no great importance, while its markings and degree of darkness are. Against this background, it is understandable that it is difficult to train dogs to colours which are usually insignificant factors in a dog's sensual world.

SENSE OF HEARING

The importance of hearing to a dog is very evident even on a very superficial acquaintance with a dog of any breed. Every active dog nearly always shows behaviour which includes an acoustic awareness of its surroundings. Social relations between dogs are based largely on the utterance of sounds, and hunting habits involve actions which to a very large extent are based on hearing.

A listening dog pricks up its ears (if their shape allows it) and naturally dogs with hanging ears use their outer ears in the same way as dogs with upright ears. When alert, they raise the base of the ear and their ears stand out more than when they are not listening. Their ability to localise a source of sound is very great. A dog swiftly turns its head so that the sound reaches both ears with the same strength, and it also rivets its gaze on the area from which the sound is coming. If it then does not succeed in seeing the source of the sound, and especially if this awakens its hunting instinct or curiosity, but no particular fear, then a dog begins to cant its head from side to side. It takes its bearings on a nearby source of sound very exactly in this way. This behaviour is also part of wolf, dog and fox behaviour in the capture of small rodents in vegetation, or when rodents move along beneath a thin layer of snow. In laboratory experiments, it has been shown that dogs and foxes can distinguish sources of sounds which, calculated from the experimental animals, lie only one degree away from each other, though this capacity to localise sounds decreases the higher the frequency.

A dog can hear sounds of every frequency and volume that a normal human being can hear, and also sounds beyond the range of the human ear. The human ear's upper unit of frequency discrimination usually lies between 16,000 and 18,000 oscillations per second (Herz). But a dog which shows no symptoms of senility can certainly hear sounds up to 30,000–40,000, and according to some sources even up to 70,000–100,000 oscillations per second. A number of neuro-physiologists, however, very much doubt that a dog can hear such extremely high notes. Perhaps one should say that dogs may react to extremely high notes, but one might well imagine a reaction to a sound, without this being taken as a distinct note. In practice, however, it is sufficient to know that in different situations a dog can hear sounds which human beings cannot.

Where is that interesting noise coming from? Localisation of a nearby source of sound is helped by canting the head.

It is not altogether easy to indicate any situation in which sensitivity to these ultra-sounds would be of great advantage to a wolf or a dog. Many small rodents' squeaks are of course so high that a considerable part of the sound falls outside human hearing. Ultra-sounds are rare among birds. But localising a source of sound which gives off only very high notes is difficult There is no evidence that a dog itself is able to make sounds which humans cannot hear. Occasionally it is maintained that dogs suffer from high notes emitting from a television set, which humans cannot hear. I have never, however, seen dogs taking the slightest notice of this sound, and neither have I been able to find the slightest deafness in my dachshunds in daily life, and they often lie quite close to the family television set. So it is hardly likely that television could cause any serious damage to a dog's hearing. Sometimes a dog reacts to technical sounds in a way that shows that the irritation to the ear is too great—it shakes its head. In nature, sounds of such strength to cause discomfort to a dog do not occur. An application of a dog's ability to hear sounds with high oscillation levels is the use of dog-whistles with notes which generally lie higher than human hearing limits.

OTHER SENSES

The reactions which the other senses of a dog release do not on the whole offer any difficulties of interpretation. A dog has tactile and pain sensations, it reacts to heat and cold, it has an evident sense of taste, and finally it also has a sense of balance which is much like ours. If you swing a dog round and round several times, it soon becomes giddy and cannot walk straight.

A dog's *sense of pain* varies. Its reactions, especially when in an aggressive mood, to something which could be presumed to cause pain are rather weak. Dogs that have been fighting cannot be separated with blows or other comparable treatment, which in fact have an almost opposite effect. (Pull them apart instead, and lift them up by their back legs.) A dog in an unaggressive mood, on the other hand, usually reacts clearly to quite insignificant painful events. Everyone must have heard how a dog squeals if one happens to tread quite lightly on its tail or paw. A mild shock of pain in what is, for an animal, a dangerous situation, can be quite beneficial. One single experience of a situation can make the animal in future always regard that situation or event with mistrust. In some higher animals which have good learning ability, the registration of accidents through a sensation of pain is naturally beneficial. The pain a dog experiences, for instance, in a fight, on the other hand, appears to add to a dog's aggressiveness and again in this way is of value. In an aggressive mood, a dog does not seem to be able to distinguish between pain caused by its opponent and that inflicted by a human's unsuccessful attempts to get the dog to stop fighting through 'punishment'.

Sometimes you get the impression that a dog reacts more to the fact that it is being punished than to the pain the punishment causes. Misjudged punishment by beating can therefore lead to a worsening of relations between master and dog—not the punisher's intention, of course. It is worth pointing out that disputes between dogs are not usually settled with sharp bites, but with display actions of different kinds. But if two dogs do in fact fight seriously, the injuries they can inflict on each other before one of them finally retreats from the field (if it can) are of such a serious nature that you naturally should never take to such brutal methods in training dogs.

A dog's *whiskers* are sense organs. In all dogs, the whiskers are situated as in wolves. The upper-lip whiskers are arranged in rows, and the lower lip's not so well developed, nor so clearly arranged. In addition, there are small groups like hairs on warts, of which two lie by the eyebrow patches, two on each cheek, one on each side of the lower jaw and one in the angle of the lower jaw. The skin of these warts contains special nerve-endings, and all whiskers are sensitive to touch. Their practical significance to a dog is, however, not often great. They have, of course, their greatest function in the dark, as for instance in a burrow.

Dogs are *sensitive to heat*. Most dogs like sunning themselves, but as soon as their coats become hot, they move into the shade. If its body temperature is raised through muscular action, a dog pants with its wet tongue hanging out, thus serving as a cooling organ, but a dog has no sweat glands with a cooling function. Panting can also be an expression of anxiety, 'nervousness', possibly followed by increased metabolism which raises the body temperature.

Sensitivity to cold in dogs expresses itself in the natural reaction of moving away from a cold area. Many dogs are definitely reluctant to go for a walk if the weather is very cold or wet. The dog indoors knows already that the weather is unfavourable.

Its sense of smell and perhaps other senses give it enough information even inside a city flat.

A dog has a well-developed sense of *taste*. It can, however, be difficult to decide whether a dog reacts primarily to taste sensations or to the smells which simultaneously appear at feeding, for instance. Even small bits of something that a dog likes can make a less favoured portion of food more attractive. A dog's reaction to different kinds of food and to some medicines which to humans have a very sharp taste, shows that dogs do not react to all tastes as humans do. Neither can the possibility be excluded that things which to humans are without smell, in fact contain sufficient scented ingredients for a dog to react to them. A dog may well find a sugar-lump because just beforehand a human had touched it. But at the same time it is not difficult to show that a dog primarily uses its vision when it is looking for a sugar-lump which has fallen on the floor. Dogs eat without hesitation strongly salted food too, salt-meat, for instance. The scent of the food is probably in such cases much more decisive to the dog than its taste.

Most domestic dogs are brought up on much the same food as we ourselves eat, but at the same time retain a dog's normal preference for all kinds of meat, bones, offal and sometimes also fish. In addition, they sometimes eat things which we humans consider repugnant. So you cannot really influence a dog's natural preference for certain foods. But at the same time, dogs show very marked individual variations when it comes to food. There are dogs, for instance, which never eat raw fish, and also those which do not even eat raw meat, unless they are starving.

It is usually not difficult to spoil a dog by always giving it food which contains what it likes most. But this only lasts as long as the dog is not starving, and is no guarantee that the dog will not suddenly and with good appetite gobble something that we think it should on no account have.

ORDER OF PRECEDENCE IN THE SENSES

Whenever a dog is on the alert, whether pronouncedly or just hinted at, it always reacts by controlling its surroundings with the three most important senses. It tries to put itself in a position in which it can use all three senses as efficiently as possible at the same time. The kind of environment and whatever the dog is occupied with at that moment determine whether the dog seeks out a more advantageous position or whether it controls the situation from where it is at the time. Details of the varying behaviour shown by the dog when it scents, hears or sees something suspicious or interesting are dealt with in combination with its instinctive actions and its social relations. Suffice it to say here that the information the dog receives from its sense of smell is much more decisive to the dog's reactions than that from its vision, and nearly always dominates that produced by its sense of hearing. A good but extreme example is the following observation made of my Scottish terrier's reactions when it suddenly saw its master dressed in a different way from usual. If at a distance it received olfactory information that this was its master, despite his strange appearance, then there were no signs of aggression. But if it was in no position to receive olfactory information, but heard his voice, it hesitated for a moment, and then ignored the unusual clothes and delightedly greeted him. Only facial features at about ten yards' distance first led to hesitant acceptance ('It's obviously the master, after all'), but before its delight took over, it first had to verify this close to with its sense of smell.

But a dog's reactions also follow another rule: a dog acts primarily according to the sense information that releases the most effective reaction, even in those cases when this information is imperfect. If neither sight nor hearing gives this information, which the dog has through earlier experience associated with strong effect, or instinctively releases very strong reactions, then it is the olfactory information which is decisive to the dog's actions. This system is naturally highly practical. It guarantees good reactions when the dog is receiving insufficient information on something which might contain danger. In an environment in which its sense of smell cannot give it sufficient information, the dog then reacts when it hears an unfamiliar noise so that it seeks out an observation point. A dog in a city flat jumps up to the window and looks round but makes no attempt to scent. On the other hand, it listens intently. On a little island, a dog is a pronouncedly visual animal, which when it hears strange sounds always looks for an observation point from which it can see as freely as possible from which direction the sound comes. Many dogs look for definite resting places out of doors. Free view in the direction from which any possible surprise, according to the dog's experience, might appear, is the most important demand made on such a place, especially if it is a dog with inclinations to keeping guard. Shelter from the wind and warmth from the sun are other factors which play a part in the choice of a resting place. In the dark, dogs which by nature are easily frightened and timid, even in familiar territory to them, can appear almost afraid of the dark. The slightest sound sends them barking and growling, until with great cautiousness and with the help of their noses and ears, they have checked that there is no danger.

2 HEREDITARY BEHAVIOUR

A dog is equipped with a wealth of different habits which in ethological language are called instinctive actions. The following brief explanation should help anyone who has little knowledge of the terminology and modern research into animal behaviour to understand what the concept of instinctive activity entails. At the same time, the release of instinctive actions is also dealt with. Anyone who wishes to go further into working methods and results of ethology should preferably acquire a brief work on modern animal psychology. Ethology and research into animal behaviour are both interesting and thought-provoking, not least because they offer us a healthy perspective of man's own behaviour.

INSTINCTIVE ACTIVITY AND ITS RELEASE

The movements which make up most animal behaviour are divided by the ethologists into two categories, fixed action patterns or instinctive activity, and 'taxes' or steering movements. 'Taxes' direct the animal's attitude (orientation) to different stimuli, for instance weight, light, sound or environmental condition, source of stimulation or some object registered by the animal. Taxes can be either inborn or acquired. Instinctive activity is such movements or actions which every member of the species in question carries out in the same way. Every species has characteristic instinctive actions and these are just as good recognition signs of the species as its anatomical and physiological characteristics, its colouring, etc. In a certain given situation, every individual in certain species acts in a typical way for its species; carries out some movement, makes some sound, etc. Every such instinctive action, which may be extremely simple or consist of a whole series of actions, can only be released by an external stimulus to this action, the 'key-stimulus' of the instinctive activity. It is said that the animal has a central nervous mechanism for every instinctive action, to which its 'key-stimulus' fits like a key in a lock. The stimulus can be of very varying kinds—visual, aural, olfactory, tactile, or a combination of several. In general, the animal reacts from birth to 'key-stimuli', but there are also instinctive actions which occur or can occur through instinctive activity that the animal does not react to from birth. In practice, it is difficult sometimes to draw a sharp line between inborn or innate releasers and those that the animal has learnt to utilise as a releaser, as there occurs an association between the carrying out of instinctive activity and a different stimulus combination from the action's innate 'key-stimulus'. In addition one and the same instinctive action can be released by several different stimuli. If a stimulus does not reach sufficient intensity to release the action, only a very little addition of one of the other stimuli is necessary for the action to be released.

If an instinctive action has not been released for a long time, but the animal's physiological condition is such that the instinctive action can be released, then the central nervous system releasing-mechanism is sensitised all the more. It is said that the threshold-value for the requisite stimulus decreases. The instinctive action can then be released by a very weak or even an incomplete stimulus, or occasionally perhaps also without visible cause, in 'a void'.

The vocalisations, movements, scents, etc., of the species are 'key-stimuli' for the instinctive actions which regulate social relations and reproduction of a species. Hostile species of different kinds release through their appearance, their movements, or some other characteristic, instinctive actions of a protective function. It is very common that an animal has developed definite markings which are revealed in a conspicuous manner when the animal carries out an instinctive action. The sight of this marking, perhaps even further revealed by some form of display, and perhaps combined with a special vocalisation, in its turn releases in another individual the same or another instinctive action.

A number of instinctive actions obviously denote pleasure—both for people and animals it is pleasant to eat, build a home, make love, and so on. The animal exhibits appetitive or searching behaviour which involves it in working towards the situations in which pleasurable instinctive actions are released. The hunting behaviour of a dog is its appetitive behaviour towards eating, but in itself, hunting behaviour is a whole series of instinctive actions, whose appetitive behaviour is the dog's effort to go off hunting.

If an instinctive movement is released again and again, it often happens that the animal begins to react more and more weakly to the stimulus which causes the action. Another adequate stimulus can, however, then still release the action with full strength. It is usually not the animal's muscles that tire, but the central nervous releasing mechanism which becomes exhausted. This phenomenon is very relevant to the fact that the animal, during its youth, or in surroundings in which the stimulus is always being repeated, gradually ceases to react to stimuli which at birth release flight, for instance, but which can be repeated without something which really appears to be dangerous appearing in the proximity of the animal. This is very important to most higher animals—it is just as important not to react unnecessarily, as it is to react properly when the need arises, and the breaking of the habit is not only concerned with flight, but also, for instance, with choice of food. It is pointless to react to everything that moves—after all, everything that moves is not prey or friendly species, and neither is it hostile. Typical of instinctive actions is that during the individual's development they gradually mature, they have a tendency to be carried out *in toto* if they are once started, they are not influenced by the processes of learning, and they are often dependent on the individual's hormonal or physiological condition.

Anyone who has known well both a male dog and a whelping bitch will have seen most instinctive actions in dogs, but probably not all. Not even a very wide experience of many different kinds of dogs guarantees that one sees all innate reactions in them. In addition, it is often quite difficult to keep the different behaviour patterns apart. In the artificial environment in which most domestic dogs and many sporting dogs live, a number of instinctive actions are so rare that they hardly ever occur, although they could be released in a relevant situation quite easily. Another point is that dog-owners do not by any means always interpret their dogs' behaviour correctly. For those with little knowledge of ethology, it is easy to see in some action an outbreak of rational behaviour, although it is in fact an instinctive action. In their right circumstances, instinctive actions do in fact often seem rational, primarily because they are then purposeful. But exactly the same behaviour can in certain cases be released in a situation in which it is not possible that it has the slightest direct significance. Then it is naturally easy to see that in each case it is a case of stereotyped behaviour which is not directed in the same way as human beings direct that part of their behaviour which is based on direct thought.

Many uninitiated people have thought that a dog is abnormal if it carries out an action in a situation in which the action is quite alien and fulfils no function. In fact in most cases, the key-stimulus exists, although the object at which the action is normally directed, or the environment in which the action becomes purposeful, does not exist. And an action which has once been started by a sufficiently strong stimulus is completed and can also be repeated until the stimulus no longer exists or is no longer effective. It may happen, too, that a link in a chain of several separate instinctive actions is released, but the key-stimulus which should release the following one does not exist. Then it looks as if a

C

fixed action pattern breaks down while in fact a whole instinctive action has been released, but not the whole series of actions which would make the action purposeful.

In situations where the stimuli exist for several different instinctive actions in which content and performance are antagonistic, it happens that some action which is quite alien to the situation in question occurs, or is perhaps indicated, while the instinctive actions whose releasers exist, do not appear at all. Such behaviour is called displacement activity. When a very happy dog bares its teeth as if it were angry, or as if it were laughing, this is typical displacement activity. The baring of teeth belongs to the functions of fighting activity, while the activities which should really have been released are licking (of the hand, or preferably the face; typical greeting behaviour) and jumping up towards the master to be able to greet him with licking. At the same time the dog is affected by an impulse not to jump up towards his master, originating from its training. In the conflict situation which arises, the baring of teeth is released. Different displacement activities are quite common in dogs. But it is not certain that every activity, which appears to us to lack adequate release, is of this type. We human beings naturally cannot by any means always notice the stimuli that can be very strong in dogs. When a dog is in a certain mood, it is especially sensitive to such stimuli which are connected with activity relevant to the function in question, but most often less sensitive to stimuli relevant to some other function and its instinctive activity. A dog which has been activated, for instance, within the function of sexual behaviour, or the function of whelping, does not react much to stimuli relevant to hunting and eating. But a bitch with activated whelping behaviour can be very aggressive, behaviour which in this case is included in the care of her whelps, but is naturally not directly related to brood-tending. So it is often difficult or impossible to separate the different so-called spheres of function completely from one another. The same movements or the same activity factor can be included in activity chains relevant to wholly different spheres of function. If the dog is deeply involved, it can happen that when it carries out the activity in question, it goes over from one sphere of function's behaviour to activity which belongs to another sphere of function. Such activity can then lead a dog's behaviour into quite different patterns. But in this case, too, one has to be cautious over drawing conclusions.

If a stimulus is very weak, it often happens that it does not release the corresponding activity completely, but just as an intention. The animal carries out first the introductory factors of the activity, and even these may be incomplete. Such behaviour is called intention movement. Naturally, it is not necessarily a matter of instinctive activity which includes a movement *sensu stricto,* but it can equally well be a matter of a sound-uttering intention. Intention movements can also be the result if the animal is affected by a stimulus while its physiological condition or its development generally does not allow the appropriate instinctive activity to occur.

Quite a large proportion of the behaviour that a dog shows in different situations are these different kinds of intention movement. These intentions have in their turn in many cases a function similar to stimuli for activity which is carried out by other individuals. One might say that the dog understands the significance of the intentions. And it swiftly learns to react to many such intention movements or activities, which it does not react to instinctively. In the life of a dog most things are regulated by encounters between different individuals with display of different kinds, and these are to a great extent intentions of fighting and flight behaviour. Also our own capacity to understand a dog's reactions and interpret its moods naturally depends on our seeing the intention movements which it carries out, and in general also interpreting them in the right way.

It is already apparent that one can start from the fact that a dog has moods which to a great extent correspond to those of humans, but naturally we cannot know exactly what a dog feels in different situations. It is probably true that these moods and their physiological background are very similar in higher mammals, including the dog and man. But only man, and perhaps also to some slight extent the primates, reflect on the reasons for moods and how one shall behave in the mood in question.

VOCALISATIONS

One does not have to have a great deal of experience to interpret most dog vocalisations in the right way. The central rôle which barking and other vocalisations play in a dog, however, indicate that they should be gone into fairly thoroughly, despite their easy comprehension. In addition, the vocalisations of dogs in certain cases are not so simply interpreted as one might think. The use of sounds not only varies individually very greatly, but also sometimes appears in a dog as displacement activity. A dog has at its command all the sounds which occur in a wolf. The differences between the sounds of a wolf and a dog are no greater than that they are due only to extensive selection carried out by man, which has led to the rise of different breeds. On the other hand, a dog's vocalisations are very different from those of both the jackal and the fox.

Barking

In most breeds, barking is the most common vocalisation. A dog barks primarily in situations which put the dog into a mood dominated by a combination of alertness-fear-aggression. Barking can appear as an intention movement, as just a weak, soundless expelling of breath. At high intensity, barking can become almost a continuous howling. The more aggression dominates, the more hollow the bark; the more the dog shows fear, the higher and more shrill becomes the bark. A dog which is not in the slightest worried only barks as a displacement activity at pleasure or if it finds itself in some special mood which is connected with sounds of the barking type, for instance at a drive or when it points game, or if it has learnt to use its bark in some special situation, for instance to draw attention to itself.

Barking in alert situations of different kinds has a clear social warning function, which man can also find useful. But a dog barks quite independently of whether it is thus warning another individual. The nuances of a bark—from strong aggression to preparation for flight—are heard by a listening dog even if it cannot see the dog that is barking, or even if the barking dog is a complete stranger. In addition the note and ring of the bark clearly tell other dogs quite a lot about the size of the barker. A small timid dog is often afraid of a deep bark, even if the barker is a long way away. A dog which knows another dog, also recognises its bark and it uses this experience on strange dogs' barks. However, it is not known whether a little dog without previous experience reacts more obviously to a large dog's bark than to a small dog's bark. This is probably unlikely; in a wolf-pack there are no drastic variations in voice and size.

Barking as an expression of joy, of expectation in face of a pleasure-denoting situation which the dog has learnt to meet, is very common. This sort of barking can sometimes be regarded as a kind of displacement activity and often also as a challenge.

Barking on drives can be regarded as a social signal, but at the same time a displacement activity. Selection has evidently greatly influenced the inclination to bark in situations relevant to hunting. In certain cases a dog barks in a situation which in natural circumstances would not give it an advantage—for instance barking at a guinea-fowl sitting high up in a tree, quite out of reach of the dog.

Although a dog's inclination to bark is usually very great, barking in an alert situation can quite easily be emphasised by training. In some examples of breeds whose bark is usually easily released, the inclination to bark in alert situations is abnormally small. Such dogs are often more aggressive and fearless than other examples of the same breed and consequently also bark less—fear is one of the most important mainsprings of barking. The popular conception that a dog which barks a lot does not bite is thus not entirely incorrect, ethologically speaking. Barking is an activity which a dog can easily learn to carry out to order, wholly independent of any innate releasing stimulus.

A dog has an inclination to bark or make itself heard in some other way when it is hindered from carrying out some worthwhile activity. This behaviour can possibly be explained by the theory of displacement activity. If the vocalisation is followed by success in the activity striven for, then the dog quickly associates its vocalisation with that success. This is, amongst other things. the reason why dogs so easily begin to bark to be given titbits.

Growling

A dog that growls deeply is demonstrating an aggressive mood which has no direct element of fear in it. But the growl does not really mean that a dog will attack. On the contrary, a dog usually growls most loudly in situations in which it is dominated by aggression, but social inhibitions stop it from attacking or biting. In this way, growling becomes a kind of demonstration of power, and it is primarily directed against enemies close to a dog and of which the dog is not afraid. At the actual moment of attack—if there is an attack—the growling usually becomes a more obvious roar. At increased intensity, growling can be stopped by short suppressed barks, without an attack following.

Another type of growling is the rather obvious intention of ordinary barking. This kind of growling easily becomes a whining or squealing sound. Naturally, there is no sharp dividing line between different types of growls. Aggressive growling can perhaps be called an intention to bark of an extreme aggressive type, which has a free-standing function and its own resonance.

Whining

A dog which has experienced some unpleasantness whines. A corresponding situation occurs if a dog is in an atmosphere in which some behaviour is strongly activated but cannot be realised. Thus one can say that both mental dissatisfaction and physically unpleasant situations cause whining. At extreme intensity, whining can easily become a sound of a barking type, and sometimes also howling. In the latter case, the reason is obviously usually discomfort of a non-physical nature.

Yelping

This sound, often a short and shrill vocalisation, is a very characteristic reaction to pain and experiences causing shock. Many dogs yelp if they are frightened by a sudden loud or unexpected noise, or something which very suddenly appears in its field of vision quite near it. Dogs with bad-tempered natures, however, do not react with any obvious yelping, but with some kind of swift flight movement, simultaneously showing signs of aggression. Dogs do not usually react to olfactory sensations with yelps, but sometimes with aggressive behaviour. Olfactory sensations hardly ever seem to appear so suddenly that they cause such a shocked reaction which, for instance, bangs or other unusual noises do. Dogs yelp if, for instance, their tails are trodden on, and often at this, in many very gentle dogs, a certain aggressive mood is released which is usually expressed by it raising its back hairs or in that it snaps quickly.

A dog's inclination to be frightened in situations of surprise varies individually a great deal. Rough dogs are not afraid, but just slightly aggressive; dogs with especially timid natures are easily frightened and cannot shake off the mood easily.

Squealing

At extreme delight and surprise, a number of dogs react by letting out a high, vibrating squealing noise. This sound appears to be released only with happiness which does not involve expectation, but satisfaction. In face of the prospect of receiving a titbit, a dog does not squeal, but when a member of the family who has been away a long time comes home, squealing occurs in an intensive greeting ceremony. A young dog occasionally squeals when it greets its mother, but the mother does not greet her pup with this sound. One gets the impression that individual dogs which seldom squeal make this sound only when they greet people or other dogs by whom they have been affected when they were pups. But there are also dogs which squeal at a quite low 'joy intensity'—or which become very happy from very insignificant causes.

Howling

In wolves, howling occurs in several different situations, but in a dog this vocalisation is not nearly so common. A wolf uses howling primarily as a kind of gathering signal in hunting. A corresponding situation is hard to find in dogs, which are, after all, not usually

Howling is released by loneliness and is clearly a rallying signal. It has a special resonance caused by the dog holding its upper lip drawn down.

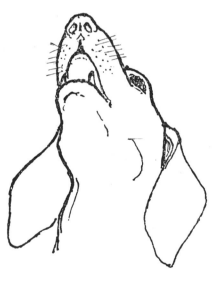

allowed to hunt in packs in extensive hunting areas in which contact between the pack's individuals is not easy to keep. In both dogs and wolves, however, howling occurs as an indication of some kind of pack feeling of affinity, the content of which has not really been closely analysed. One animal begins to howl and the others soon follow suit. It is often easy to get a dog to howl quite loudly by using this reaction. Humming and playing music of different kinds releases howling in some dogs. Dogs used to music hardly react at all, while dogs who have never heard music are considerably more sensitive. One can cause howling most easily by directly imitating the howl of a dog. Presumably dogs can show some kind of emotion which corresponds to grief, but that they should then howl is unlikely. On the other hand, it is more likely that desertion and loneliness release howling as a kind of gathering signal. Also, a hunting wolf which loses contact with members of the pack naturally also falls into such a mood and starts howling. According to this argument, howling would not really be a gathering signal, but in certain situations it might acquire this significance. There are also examples of very sudden joy giving rise to short but intensive howling.

OTHER VOCALISATIONS; UNDERSTANDING THE
SIGNIFICANCE OF VOCALISATIONS

The vocalisations of dogs are far from stereotyped and variations in their use occur very often. *Intermediate forms between two or more vocalisations* are in a number of dogs more usual than vocalisations which indicate a 'pure' mood. Dogs also have a very great capacity for reacting to each other's vocalisations according to the mood content that such a mixed vocalisation has. It is quite common that a dog barking at something makes another dog bark at something quite different. Under the influence of the bark from the other dog, a dog may believe, if one may use a somewhat anthropomorphic expression, that some object which is in reality quite harmless is dangerous. One can express roughly the same thing more scientifically: the bark releases a mood which lowers the threshold value for the stimuli that can release reactions of fear or make the dog look for reasons in its environment for the barking of the other dog.

Growling is associated with marked facial expressions which presumably at close quarters are more effective signals than the sound itself. I shall return to facial expressions in another context later. Also, growling can in another dog release reactions of fear of quite harmless sounds or objects. But growling is primarily directed at another dog nearby which in its turn does not misunderstand this vocalisation. But it can happen that the *nasal sounds* unnatural to a dog, which a number of pug-type dogs make when they are happy or excited, are misunderstood by dogs which have not previously come into contact with these strange and incomprehensible vocalisations of mood. These sounds have caused clear suspicious-aggressive behaviour in my dachshunds, amongst others. Naturally these nasal sounds have no clear ethological significance. Their mood content is quite unknown to other dogs, and possibly even to them themselves.

Many dogs make a *weak crooning* sound when in a friendly mood. Since her infant days, my old dachshund bitch has 'cooed' at each indrawn breath when she is very happy, especially when she is calmly moving around out of doors. Indoors, she only makes this sound now and again when in a satisfied mood. The inclination to make this sound, which is not part of instinctive behaviour, is to some extent hereditary. Of my dachshund's ten pups, two have had the same inclination, though rather weak. It is in all probability caused by some unimportant anatomical anomaly. The sound occurs in roughly the same way as a snore. The way the muscles in the region of the larynx and throat tighten and loosen in different moods leads to the sound occurring in certain moods, while it does not occur in other moods.

Dogs can *sigh* very markedly. A dog which has settled down sighs when after much scratching and turning it has at last got comfortable. Dogs sigh when, after having great expectations, they finally give up hope that the expected will happen. Dogs which are very contented but not excited often sigh, provided they are sitting still or lying down, preferably on someone's knee. A dog's inclination to sigh is especially evident if a member of the family who has been away a long time allows the dog uninhibitedly to greet him and then sit on his lap. The dog's facial expression in this situation is one of 'bliss'. One cannot say that sighing has any real ethological function. It is clear, however, that dogs and people sigh in rather similar moods. Physiologically the sigh can be called a deep compensatory inspiration of breath after a strain that may lower the breathing tempo, or directly increase the need for oxygen, through mental strain.

Dogs begin to *sneeze* if they lie on their backs with their noses pointing upwards. Evidently a fluid from the breathing tubes in the nostrils irritates the scent membranes.

Coughing is common in dogs, sometimes in the form of short spurts of air much like our own cough, but also another kind which causes a hooting sound on inspiration, which is repeated with a number of cramp-like breaths following one another, then slowly dying down. In breathing of this kind, expiration occurs swiftly and without coughing interruptions. The dog appears sick and it all looks very unpleasant, but the coughing spell vanishes quickly by itself. The cause of this cramp-like breathing appears to be irritants in the bronchial tubes. My dachshunds usually have this trouble when they have been digging in loose dry soil. Sneezing, on the other hand, does not result from this kind of digging. It can be mentioned that these reflex-released sounds have no social function and are not noticed much by surrounding dogs.

Dogs often *snore* very loudly, and older dogs snore more than younger ones. Not even the loudest snore releases reactions in other dogs except, at the most, a feeble passing surprise.

COLOUR-MARKINGS, EXPRESSIONS AND MOVEMENTS AS SOCIAL SIGNALS

Wolf expressions of mood and display involving facial expressions, postures and movements are retained practically unchanged in a dog, and wolf behaviour has been investigated quite thoroughly, so most of the results of this analysis thus can also be applied to dogs, or at least to those dogs which have an anatomical pre-disposition to carry out the same actions as the wolf. A dog, how-ever, does not carry out the same actions with the same precision as a wolf. A dog without a tail naturally cannot wag its tail; a dog with soft pendulous ears cannot give such clear expressions of changing moods as a wolf can. A dog with long facial hair hides the many finesses of facial expression behind a bushy beard and long chap-hairs. In a number of breeds, facial skin is so taut that facial expressions are influenced, and in others the face has such thick rolls of loose skin that expressions cannot change easily. Large individual differences within one and the same breed also exist. So one can say that every dog is to a certain extent a special individual, but at the same time there are common features which are easy to identify.

The scutcheon

The scutcheon or perineal region is the most characteristic marking in dogs of many different breeds and in wolves of all colours. It is nearly always sharply demarcated and light, and the fact that the perineal region is so constant has a natural explanation. In the social behaviour of the animal in question, this region is of extreme significance as the centre of scents of individual character and social function. The prominence caused by the colour differing from that of the surrounding hairs is fully compatible with the principles which generally prevail in the origin and accentuation of markings with strong signalling functions. In wolves of some colour types, the perineal region is optically strengthened by the light and dark part of the sides of the thighs and tail. A dog often has an evenly dark part across its haunches and thighs. The contrast between the light scutcheon and the otherwise dark haunches is then very clear. Many black or brown dogs have a white or light yellow perineal region.

Other colour-markings

The other colour characteristics which are found in wolves of most colour types and which also appear in many dogs are the light markings on the throat (or the whole chest) and on the lips and cheeks, often in combination with light eyebrow-patches and dark markings round the eyes. This dark marking has a certain tendency to remain in breeds which have white on their noses and a white blaze. Facial markings also naturally have a certain significance. You could say that a facial marking of the type described above and a light perineal region constitute a kind of basis marking in dogs in general. That a number of breeds do not have these markings shows that they are not impossible to eliminate. At the same time, it is clear that they have a very strong tendency to remain in dogs whose markings in other respects are not similar to those of wolves.

Eye-patches can at least be presumed to function as markers for the direction of the eyes. In weak light, it is not easy to see the direction in which the nose of an alert wolf or dog is pointing. So in a pack, these light eye-patches make the individual's reactions to each other easier. If the eye-patches can perhaps occasionally serve as detractors for attacks directed at eyes, I waive this judgement.

Expressions

Lips, the eye region, ears and to a certain extent the eyes, together form a mechanism with a wealth of opportunities for expression. With these optical opportunities, with its movements and its acoustic signalling system, a dog gives its environment—other dogs as well as people—a very diversified picture of the moods by which at each separate moment it is dominated. It is not easy to describe all the combinations in a dog's expression, so we shall have to be content with an outline of the basic types of expressions. If you know them, it is not so difficult to analyse those which make up a dog's facial expression in each separate situation—most of all if you know the breed, and preferably also the individual dog in question.

Aggression

The most easily recognisable expression a dog can show, and for humans the most important for practical reasons, is signs of aggression. It is said that a dog bares its teeth. But there are several details in aggressive behaviour which show the degree

A dog's expression at strong aggression (above), at pronounced fear (right), and in a mood which contains both aggression and fear (left).

of aggression. Let us, however, first presume that the dog does not show the slightest trace of fear, and consequently that the dog's expression in fact shows a tendency to pure aggression of different degrees of motivation. In such a purely aggressive mood, the ears are always raised—pricked—and clearly forward, but they are not noticeably drawn inwards towards each other across the forehead. Hanging ears are held in a corresponding manner with the base of the ears strongly outwards, so the hanging part stands out as far as possible. The greater the aggression is, the higher the dog lifts its upper lip round its front and canine teeth, more so on the side that is facing 'the enemy'. At the same time the upper part of the nose is wrinkled. In an extreme mood, the tip of the nose is turned noticeably upwards, at which very clear wrinkles appear across the nose. Wrinkles also appear round the eyes and lengthwise along the head. The skin is drawn in the direction of the eyes and eyebrow-patches, where a strong ridge of skin appears. This wrinkling also appears, however, in a defensive attitude, and consequently when the dog is prepared to bite but not attack. The wrinkles round the mouth and tip of the nose are, on the other hand, only aggressive. In pure aggression, the corners of the mouth are never drawn right back, but the mouth is short in profile.

In an aggressive mood, the dog raises the hair along the centre of its spine from its shoulders to the middle of its tail. Most powerfully, it raises the hairs between its shoulder-blades and on its lower back. With extreme aggression, the hairs on these parts rise within two to five seconds after the dog has seen something agitating, but with mild aggression it takes up to thirty seconds before this hormonally released reaction appears. The hairs remain raised for some time after the dog has calmed down in other respects, but as long as the hairs are raised, the dog is more than usually prepared to behave aggressively in situations when in normal circumstances it would not do so. My dachshunds defend, for instance, a sugar-lump as long as their back hairs are raised, but not otherwise.

In a wolf, the centre line of the spine and tail is dark. A wolf which raises its back hairs thus emphasises this dark part and also the animal in this way looks larger and more imposing. Dogs often have backs all one colour, but the raised ridge of hairs on a smooth-haired dog's back appears as a dark band if the dog is not very light.

A marked steadiness in its gaze is also one of the features which are typical of a dog in a fiercely aggressive mood. A dog which is afraid does not stare at its antagonist in the same pronounced manner.

Fear

The other type of mood which stamps the behaviour of dogs in daily life is different degrees of fear. In most cases, however, it is a case of brief moments of uncertainty or inferiority, feelings of unpleasantness of very meagre strength. Such strong fear that gives rise to, for instance, flight away from equals, or possible real enemies of different kinds, is exceptional, both in wolves and in dogs. It is worth pointing out that too easily released flight can be of great detriment to a dog. Flight from equals is often quite aimless and also flight can release chasing, in other words an action which is part of hunting behaviour and which released by the same species can have undesirable consequences.

A frightened dog does not keep its ears pricked and forward if the danger is not far away, and the dog's behaviour is thus only dominated by attention to danger. In extreme fear, on the other hand, the ears are always laid backwards and at the same time the corners of the mouth are drawn far back. The dog's whole face appears drawn out and narrow in contrast to the compact stubby expression in a very aggressive dog's face. In general, however, a not very marked, but quite clearly fearful mood is combined with preparations for defence. This defence preparation is demonstrated by a certain wrinkling of the forehead, but the lips and tip of the nose are not raised so demonstrably as in purely aggressive moods, and thus the baring of the teeth is less marked. The more the uncertainty grows, i.e. the greater and/or more threatening the opponent is, the more clearly the lips are drawn back, the further back go the ears (if the ears are of the upright kind) and the smoother the forehead and skull become. With very great fear, the ears of all dogs lie quite flat.

A dog dominated by aggression makes small jerks forward with its head at back height, its nose slightly downwards and its front legs slightly apart. A frightened dog has a tendency to bend its back, lower its haunches and raise its nose a little. This can be described as a position of self-defence. A dog with this expression can, if it suddenly becomes even more frightened, even squeal. A lesser degree of aggression, especially in smaller dogs, is expressed in yapping, which at a high intensity can pass into a miserable whine.

In an aggressive mood inhibited by fear, many dogs make snapping intentions to bite. Their teeth are bared for a moment and their jaws rattle against each other.

The face and ears often look very different in different breeds. So it is difficult to describe simply all the different combinations which facial expressions can have. Naturally you soon learn from experience your own dog's expressions, but this does not mean that from this you can always judge a strange dog's mood too. I have personal experience of this. During my earliest childhood years there were always Dobermanns in our house, and as I grew up, a dachshund and then later three Scotties. Dobermanns and dachshunds have largely indentical expressions, although the dachshund has long ears. But at first the Scotties caused a certain amount of trouble. Their tails and ears did not 'tell' us enough, as we were used to seeing the actual facial expression in the short-haired breeds. Several controversies between the Scotties and other dogs, and between the Scotties and children would have been avoided if we had immediately been able to read the Scotties' moods as well as we could our other dogs'. Now that I have dachshunds again, I can only confirm that despite its many pleasant characteristics and its piquant appearance, the Scottie must be described as very hard to understand. Anyone wishing to study the changes of mood of his dog should preferably not choose one with long facial hair. But this should naturally not be taken as a judgement of those breeds which have long facial hair. They are excellent in many ways, but not entirely suitable for an ethologist!

D

Tail

Next to its expressions and vocalisations, a dog's tail is the best
indicator of its mood. There are, however, dogs which scarcely
move their tails at all, and naturally in these cases the tail tells you
nothing of their mood. As far as the use of the tail as a signal for
different moods is concerned, our knowledge is largely based on the
study of wolves, but naturally that causes few difficulties when
studying the dog's use of its tail. A wolf has a much more expressive
use of its tail than a dog. The greatest difference is the wolf's
tendency not to raise its tail or wag it unnecessarily. But the main
point is that the wolf also, in special moods, eagerly wags its tail and
it can also lift its tail high, as for instance, an Alsatian does. Domestication has obviously influenced the dog's way of holding its tail
and the inclination itself to wag it more than it has influenced basic
facial expressions. It is said that the difference between a wolf and
an Alsatian can already be seen at a distance; the wolf does not hold
its tail erect, the Alsatian does. This difference, however, is only
partly due to a certain difference in the manner of using the tail in
different moods. In identical external circumstances, a wolf and a
dog naturally find themselves in extremely different moods. When
a person happens to see a wild wolf, the wolf is frightened, aggressive or tired. An Alsatian is seldom in these moods and holds its tail
accordingly. At the same time, there are also quite marked
differences in moods of wolves and dogs. Domestication has meant
that the average dog has a less aggressive and more playful
temperament than the wolf, and a dog's tail movements are
naturally related to its temperament. For most of the time it is
moving, a dog, especially if it is with people, is obviously happy
and friendly. It wags its tail much more for people, most of
all its owners, than for other dogs. But even to its equals, a
dog wags its tail much more than a wolf does to its equals. There
is no obvious anatomical difference which would hinder the wolf
from lifting its tail high, but it appears that a dog's tail is usually
more muscular at the base than a wolf's. This difference might

have something to do with why a dog wags its tail so much more than a wolf does.

Wagging its tail is a dog's most important greeting action and demonstration of friendliness. Less well known is that wagging even occurs in quite different moods. A trembling movement of the tail held very high means an extremely aggressive, or at least dominant, mood. A dog making this movement, as far as I have been able to see, is always very superior to its antagonist. When seeking out prey, which a dog does primarily with its sense of smell, for instance when looking for small mammals, and when a sporting dog is looking for the scent of game, a special kind of wagging occurs. The tail is then held far more upright and the beat of the wagging is smaller. Instead, the movement is much swifter. Expectation of being allowed to carry out some hunting activity (catching prey, shaking it to death) may well be expressed in the form of this movement. A dog also wags its tail in situations in which it expects something especially attractive, from its owner or from another dog for instance, but then the movement is simultaneously a demonstration of friendliness.

Both in dogs and wolves, a strange jerky movement occurs of the outer part of the tail, which is stretched straight out, or to the side. Tails of a number of breeds, however, are shaped so that this movement is not very prominent. It is something like the way a cat moves its tail when it is extremely angry. The fox, too, has the same way of jerking its tail when in an aggressive mood.

The safer and more unafraid a dog feels when near another dog, the higher it raises its tail. The tail is, however, also 'speaking' when no other dogs are around. Relations between dog and owner are reflected continuously in the position and movements of the dog's tail, as what the dog is expecting will happen through the owner's or other people's behaviour. A dog's own state of health is also reflected in the way it moves its tail. A dog that tends to hold its tail lower than horizontal mostly feels inferior or in some other way in a bad mood, either tired, or ill or out of sorts for some special reason. When a dog holds its tail between its legs, on the other hand, it is then extremely frightened. This may be a question of preparation for flight or a demonstration of inferiority to a larger dog or a possibly dangerous person. Tail-wagging occurs, however, at all tail positions. And if the wags are not of the swift hunting type, or the jerky highly aggressive type or the trembling type, then they are always a sign that the dog's mood contains a larger or smaller proportion of something which lies between the most violent joy and abject submission.

If tail-wagging occurs in a clearly frightened mood, it is combined with more or less bent back and lowered haunches. The tail is held very low and wags in a way which one can best describe as timidly and submissively. The whole of the hind region of the body can wag too in this trembling wagging. Simultaneously the head is often held on a slant and the dog makes intentions of lying on its back. The drawn-back mouth, flattened ears and submissive flickering eyes mean that in this mood the dog portrays complete humility and definitive submission. In extreme cases, a dog holds its tail between its legs and at the same time eagerly wags it. Younger dogs in this mood often show an inclination to begin playing, but the picture of submissiveness becomes in this way even more obvious. Play is then the opposite of aggression.

The position of the tail is also influenced by other moods than those mentioned so far. The following tail characteristics refer to dogs which do not hold their tail constantly arched over their backs. An eating dog holds its tail stretched out backwards and downwards and immobile in a characteristic manner. A dog which is carrying a bone about usually holds its tail slightly higher, giving the impression that it is 'food-holding' combined with a somewhat clearer inclination to defence. One can perhaps call this a mood of proud right of possession. This position is quite independent of whether a person or a rival for the bone is present. A bitch which in a calm mood carries a pup in her mouth, holds her tail stretched out but not raised, at the same time holding her neck high with her nose more or less horizontal. At the slightest aggression, or if the bitch is disturbed during this activity, her tail rises, but simultaneously she at once puts down the pup. A dog, which with the help of its sense of smell analyses some object which does not rouse aggressive associations, holds its tail stretched out straight. At sexual invitation, a bitch turns her tail sharply to the side, either low or high. This tail position is an anatomical condition for mating, but has a clear signalling function.

A humble dog hides its perineal region and its conspicuous markings below the lower tail. An aggressive dog, on the other hand, demonstrates its scutcheon by holding its tail up. At a distance, tail movements are also a dog's most visible signals. In addition to this, the fact that the movements may increase the actual spreading of scents when dogs confront one another, may well have added to the origins of tail movements.

Expressions of other moods

Other moods besides those connected with aggression or fear are also expressed in a dog's facial expression. A number of such moods, however, are reflected so weakly that they may be hard to see in dogs you do not know well. It can, for instance, be a question of a combination of an alert mood and friendliness, or an alert mood with no trace of the insecurity which is most often found when the dog is alerted to events slightly further away. Eyes, ear position, facial features, tail movements, breathing and posture change very sensitively, and the spectator cannot in only one of these indicators see all the changes in a dog's mood, even in calm domestic conditions. Two moods under normal domestic circumstances, however, have easily described characteristics, and they are the extremely contented and calm mood, and the challenge to play.

The calm satisfied mood in a number of dogs has a special sign which can here be called *a smile*. When it is calm and contented and satisfied with all and sundry, a dog with sufficiently mobile skin at the corners of its mouth then gets a small crease just by or above the angle of the mouth. In alert situations, this smile vanishes at once, but if the dog likes being stroked, the smile increases at calm stroking of the head and back, or scratching of the neck or stomach. The slightest sign of social insecurity makes the smile vanish, as does the slightest anxiety or expectation, even if the latter is something emphatically positive. In a weak joyful mood,

Dogs with loose facial skin in a contented, calm mood produce a characteristic crease at the corner of the mouth—the dog is 'smiling'.

for instance when its owner comes into the room and the dog wags its tail once or twice, the smile may remain or even become more obvious. A dog that smiles is clearly a very happy dog, but it is not excited or prepared to play. My dachshunds show clear smiles when they first have wildly greeted the homecoming member of the family and are then allowed to sit on the person's knee. This smile is then combined with flattened ears, eyes half-open and fixed on the object of their delight so that the whites show in the corners. The nose points slightly upwards and sighs complete the mood expressions. Another situation when a smile appears in my dachshunds is the extremely friendly and slightly expectant mood aimed at getting someone to go out into the kitchen to cook the food. Thus in this mood, too, the most important factor is a very great satisfaction, especially if the reason for that satisfaction is something which will happen after a while. In this situation, however, the ears are not laid back, but demonstratively held outwards and the forehead is slightly wrinkled. Thus this behaviour shows very clear features of invitation.

A dog's general posture and manner of carrying out different movements is also an expression of different moods. A dog performs a kind of display activity, which consists of carrying out different movements a trifle more powerfully, more slowly and more definitively than usual. In this way, a dog demonstrates its strength and size to its antagonist. In fighting, this demonstration can become complete immobility, at which a dog holds its muscles at full tension, growls, and, if it is the stronger, stares at its opponent. Stiffening into a position which includes a demonstration of inferiority (head turned aside) also occurs. These ceremonies will be dealt with more fully in connection with the rank order behaviour of dogs.

Both in fully grown dogs, young dogs and older pups, behaviour occurs which quite rightly is called play. Dogs' manner of inviting one another to this behaviour is easily recognised and is part aggressive and part submissive, paraded with great attention. Dogs' games will be dealt with in connection with the development of pups. All that need be said here is that a dog which invites another smaller or weaker dog than itself to play, usually holds its ears even nearer to each other than in a purely aggressive mood, and included in a subordinate dog's play invitation is often the 'frightened' ear position paraded with a quite fearless tail position and no fear in the eyes. But it does happen that a dominant dog when inviting to play emphasises its goodwill to a weaker partner by holding its ears well back.

Can dogs misunderstand one another?

Under normal circumstances, dogs very rarely misunderstand the content of each other's behaviour. Breeds which hide most of their facial expressions and perhaps even their tails and ears in a thick coat, are also understood quite well by dogs of other breeds. Obviously dogs do not place much importance in details of expression, but react to the total impression the opposite number makes. If, for instance, the baring of teeth doesn't show, an opponent will still perceive the dog's aggression and will react accordingly. We, however, do not see what to it appears a definite indication of mood. Thus there are double and more safeguards in the social relations of dogs. This can easily be shown by lifting the lip of a dog which is not at all aggressive and seeing what another dog 'says' about this grimace. At most, there may be an annoyed bark, but not at all the strong reaction this grimace would have released if the dog had been really angry. In many cases, social relations of dogs are determined by the knowledge they have learnt from earlier confrontations with each other. In this way, all possibility of misunderstanding is avoided. But dogs who have no experience of each other do not in general misunderstand each other either.

There is, however, one special source of misunderstanding, and that is when a dog has had a definite and very conspicuous experience, perhaps involving fear, of a certain individual dog's behaviour. Dogs of the same breed as that connected with this experience can thus release the same reaction at first even when their mood would not cause it at all. Both my dachshunds are afraid of Airedale terriers because a certain Airedale bitch has been repeatedly aggressive towards them. Such lessons tend to remain a long time and are naturally of biological significance, even if they sometimes have annoying consequences for a dog-owner. They may, for instance, mean that dogs which should not be negatively disposed towards each other can never be friendly.

REACTIONS TO PREY AND FOOD

Hunting behaviour

The wolf's interest in the most varying kinds of prey remains to a very great extent in a number of dog breeds, even if hunting behaviour itself is perhaps not so efficient as in the wolf. In most dog breeds with a definite hunting interest, efficient hunting actions are adapted only for certain categories of prey, or for certain kinds of sport. So man has influenced a dog's hunting behaviour to a great extent through conscious or unconscious selection. In those breeds which have specialised hunting behaviour, however, a weak interest remains for 'undesirable' categories of prey. By chance this interest can be increased in a disturbing manner. But one can, through training, at least largely eliminate the consequences of such undesirable interest. In breeds which normally have a very marked hunting interest, however, there are some dogs which are almost completely uninterested in all forms of hunting. They perhaps react for a moment to a track or a scent, but do not complete the action which the scent releases. Perhaps it has happened that during breeding, or at least during a period of the breed history, there has been too much emphasis on a certain external appearance or a certain temperament, and hunting skill may have suffered. Modern breeders of sporting dogs pay a great deal of attention to skills for different purposes. So there is no need to worry that the faults of the past will be repeated.

It is very possible that many of the larger breeds have a sufficiently complete set of instinctive actions for the catching of prey that these dogs put in the same situation as a young wolf in wild circumstances would learn to catch prey in the same way as wolves do. That hunting interest even in the most domesticated of dogs has not disappeared entirely, is part of the most elementary behaviour of animals.

The wolf has several different hunting-behaviour patterns. These all exist in at least some dog breeds, and many breeds still have several of them very well maintained. The actions of a wolf when it tears at large prey are naturally rare in dog behaviour, for a dog is generally not allowed to attack large mammals. But dogs which have been used to chase away baboons from crops, to judge from descriptions, behave much like wolves hunting reindeer for instance. Clear traces of this behaviour can also be seen when larger dogs bark at cattle or elk. But the important impulse for hunting, that of biting the hind leg or the throat, is fortunately weak. There are hardly any investigations into the existence and completeness of the latter in dogs.

It seems likely to me that the ability to 'point' game may originate from hunting behaviour of the wolf when hunting in a pack. Whilst one member of the pack attracts the prey's attention to itself, the others have an opportunity to make decisive moves such as catching the prey by the leg or in the belly. Pointing barking at squirrels or forest birds, for instance, is a highly unlikely activity in an experienced wolf, but an inexperienced animal might well be interested in such prey which is quite out of reach. It is man who has made the pointing of quite unreachable game into a direct advantage for the hunting dog and it has obviously been easy to increase this disposition by selection. There is, however, another factor which is significant when it comes to pointing. A dog barks very easily in situations in which it can see but cannot reach something which is very desirable.

A strong inclination to bark without any notable aggression or obvious fear is typical of, amongst others, pointers, which of course are also inclined to go for guinea-fowl and squirrels in trees. This dog obviously finds it easy to associate the different events with each other which lead to such a prey being shot: the dog barks, the person comes, shoots the prey and rewards the dog. Starting from individual features of temperament and the ability to associate, it has been possible to produce dogs with a very great inclination to bark at game. That such dogs also bark in situations when it is not wholly agreeable that it does so, can be a less desirable by-product of breeding principles.

Dogs of different breeds have a very varied inclination to *pointing game that 'freezes'*. This reaction is not very obvious in wolves, but the behaviour pattern which has been exploited by breeding clearly exists in at least most wild canines. One can divide the original behaviour pattern into three phases. Faced with a scent which seems to come from some very close point, the animal stops and tries to locate the origin of the scent, first with its sense of smell, but also with the help of its other senses. The second phase is that the animal slowly moves in the direction of a fairly thoroughly localised prey, without the animal's movement causing the prey to fly away—it is usually birds in question with this kind of behaviour. The third phase is a direct attack on the localised prey. Man has tried to eliminate the latter phase, and to develop the creeping activity as much as possible. Faced with a predator, guinea-fowl and some wildfowl react by freezing into absolute immobility. Predators have in fact little ability to localise a 'freezing' bird, or for that matter a 'freezing' hare or a broody guinea-fowl on her nest. Their scent is clearly very weak. If the predator normally possessed the same ability to kill 'freezing' game as the hunting pair, dog-plus-armed-man, then the reaction of freezing when faced with predators would not have developed. Thus, by shooting or catching the prey the dog is pointing, man has made this way of hunting considerably more successful than it is for a lone predator. But it has obviously not been difficult to achieve through selection dogs highly suited to this kind of hunting.

Another type of behaviour associated with nearby prey, is that the predator stands immobile and carefully tries to lie down in a prepared position. If the prey then approaches, a swift attack follows with an attempt at biting. This behaviour is very marked in the wolf and is quite clear in most dogs, in those never used for hunting, too. I should think that the wolf and the dog show this behaviour primarily in situations in which they can see the prey very well, but the prey does not react to the predator, or even see it. This behaviour is also used very often in connection with play and as display behaviour, of which more later.

A dog, like a wolf, and especially a fox, catches small game which it has localised but cannot see, with a very special action: the so-called Vole jump (*Mäusesprung* in German). The dog stands quite immobile and listens, fixing its eyes on the point in the vegetation from which the animal's sound is coming, and then suddenly jumps high up, at which its forelegs and nose are held close together and the back bent. The dog tries in this way to knock the prey down with its forepaws and simultaneously catch it in its jaws. *Lesser prey* which a dog has succeeded in catching is *shaken* with great force— often it is this shaking and not the bite itself which kills animals such as voles. Shaking also occurs as an extremely rough demonstration of power in fighting, and as one of the most common actions in play with different objects.

Prey which suddenly jumps up and runs away in front of a dog almost infallibly releases a *chase reaction* and hunting behaviour associated with the catching of prey, or at least an attempt to bite it. The reaction to chase prey is the reason why dogs react to children for instance, who run past them, passing motor-cycles, etc. When the dog once reacts, it may also have an impulse to bite without being aggressive in the essential meaning of the word—a latent danger which a dog-owner should be aware of.

Other hunting behaviour is primarily of interest from a purely hunting point of view. This aspect is dealt with in cynological hunting literature and has no special reference to the ethological characteristics of the dog.

Taking away of food

A dog's reaction to food involves behaviour which to a great extent illuminates what is stereotyped in a dog's way of reacting.

When in the presence of another dog, a dog receives a large piece of meat or some other food which it can carry, it takes it in its mouth and moves a bit away before it begins eating. A person's presence also releases this action. The function of this behaviour is naturally to rescue the food from rivals. If several wolves are simultaneously eating off the same prey, then if every individual had the inclination to take pieces to safety, the weaker would soon lose their pieces to the stronger. A dog or a wolf which is eating a piece itself, however, is not likely to steal food from others, so long as the desired piece is not clearly larger than its own piece, and so long as the other piece's owner is not weaker and less aggressive than the first. Dogs do not mind sharing a food-bowl, partly because they cannot take their own bowls with them so that other dogs cannot see what they are eating. If you give a dog an opened tin, for instance, it is likely to take the tin a few yards to one side before it starts licking the contents. The larger the object the dog is given, the greater the inclination to carry the object 'to safety' before it can begin to eat.

Hiding of food

Meat-eating animals bury their food to avoid rivalry from carrion-eaters, or to lessen the competition from their fellows, and perhaps also so that the food shall not lie in strong sunlight, open to infection from flies, for instance. Canines and felines generally bury food, and felines may also drag food up into trees, and in the Scandinavian bird world the hiding of food occurs generally among crows and rooks and similar birds. By hiding remains of its prey the wolf avoids the competition which ravens and other carrion-eating birds would constitute. The wolf cannot entirely hide its food from its equals and other mammals by burial, but naturally the possibility of its fellows finding the food is lessened if it is buried. Buried food naturally cannot give off such a clear scent as food lying openly on the ground.

An obviously hungry dog usually does not bury bones or other food. Not until the dog has had sufficient to eat is the food-hiding reaction released. It may happen, however, that a dog which is offered several bones at the same time, does not begin to eat them at all, but hides most or all of them, despite the fact it has not eaten for several hours. I have the impression that a dog which has often hidden bones, associates this obviously very powerful effect 'hide bone' so strongly with the situation 'get bone' that this activity is also released when the dog has not eaten nearly sufficient, or is even quite hungry. Complete satisfaction can sometimes inhibit hiding, for a satisfied dog is strongly inclined to lie down and sleep. Bone-hiding, or hiding food in general, can be released regardless of whether there is another dog nearby or not. I have, however, many times noticed that another dog's presence lessens the inclination to hide food. There is a certain contradictory element between hiding and defending food, whilst the defending and eating of food merge with each other. Dogs which defend bones they have buried, according to this often dig up the bone in association with defence behaviour, and often also begin to eat the bone.

On his way to hide a bone. The dog's posture shows preparedness and its mood will easily pass to aggression, in which case its hiding-behaviour will be interrupted.

A dog in a bone-hiding mood (or other food which can easily be carried) behaves very characteristically. It slowly takes the bone in its mouth and wanders 'carefully' away with a stiff but not markedly erect tail. One might say that the dog looks purposeful, although it by no means heads for any definite place. Simultaneously, it has certain aggressive features and adopts thus a display posture. But if its aggressiveness increases so much that it raises its hackles, the bone-hiding mood vanishes at once, and the dog begins to gnaw the bone.

A dog's bone-hiding activity is released primarily by food that is not especially desirable, but strangely enough, most dogs are not inclined to bury food that might be called artificial. This activity is primarily released by raw meat and bones of varying sizes, but not by such small pieces that do not take up the whole of the dog's mouth. Pieces of food of a size that have to be carried away so as not to rouse a rival's interest are thus a main prerequisite. Small pieces of food, on the other hand, are eaten immediately in a competitive situation. Food which is not difficult to divide or crush, but which hangs out of the mouth, like fish, for instance, is also often buried. On the other hand I have never seen dogs bury bits of bread or other fairly soft food made by humans, but according to some sources this may occasionally happen. Hiding behaviour is thus released primarily in a situation in which the dog is not immediately able to eat food which it can carry in its mouth. This behaviour is strongly stimulated by animal food and obviously mostly by food that smells of raw meat. The disposition to bury food clearly has much the same releasers as the inclination to defend food. The strength of the cause of this activity need not necessarily be in direct relation to the food's desirability.

There are dogs which harbour a great desire for chocolate, and the younger of my dachshunds is one of these. She has since her earliest youth loved chocolate more than most foods which include meat, and even more than bones, to judge from her facial expression and behaviour when she eats these foods. But she does not defend a piece of chocolate. I can take a piece of chocolate out of her mouth, but I cannot remove even the smallest piece of sun-dried bone or a minute piece of meat without her resisting me. The difference also shows clearly in her inclination to defend chocolate and meat against her much stronger mother.

To summarise, it can be said that both defence and hiding behaviour are primarily stimulated by natural meat foods, and hiding behaviour presumes in addition that the dog cannot hide the whole piece of meat in its mouth. Severe hunger inhibits hiding behaviour, as does aggressive competition from other dogs.

Actual *hiding behaviour* is extremely stereotyped and entails several phases, the first of which is the search for a suitable place, but the suitability is something highly diffuse. When the hiding mood has been released, in certain cases the most astonishingly unsuitable places seem to suffice for the completion of the actions. When dogs are to hide food out of doors, they perhaps learn the very first time where it is practical to dig a hole. The dog tries digging in several places before it finally finds a congenial place where the ground is soft. The place should preferably be to one side, under a bush or near a large stone.

But indoors, this activity is carried out in the most unsuitable places. The dog seeks out an angle between a piece of furniture and a wall, for instance, or jumps up on upholstered furniture and begins to dig with its forepaws. Some kind of hidden, soft under-layer is clearly a releasing stimulus for the second phase of hiding. In soft ground, the dog digs with subdued speed, but with great strength, a hole about the size of its muzzle, into which it slowly lays the bone. During the actual digging, the bone or piece of food in question lies just beside the dog's forelegs, so the dog never lets the food out of its sight for one moment whilst it is digging. The bone is then pushed into the hole with the nose. Then the dog presses its nose repeatedly against the bone or pushes it with his nose. Even when the bone is placed on a fairly hard underlayer, for instance in a cranny on a rug, the dog makes these pushing movements with its nose. Then follows the covering of the bone. The dog pushes its nose from all directions along the surface of the earth and in this way replaces the dug up material over the bone. Untouched material from the ground within a radius of about twelve to eighteen inches also falls on the bone, and if the lower layer has been suitable, traces of digging are finally hardly visible. As long as the dog's nose is directly touching the bone whilst it is pushing it and also pressing the surface material over it, the dog goes on shovelling with its nose. If the bone-hiding activity goes on indoors, naturally this activity does not lead to any result. Not even a soft rug can be made to cover a bone with nose movements, and the result is in most cases that the dog picks the bone up after a while and either repeats the hiding actions in another place, or begins to gnaw the bone. On the other hand, in this mood, dogs very rarely leave the bone.

Thus it can be seen that the dog carries out actions which are included in food-hiding even in a situation in which there is nothing for the dog to dig a hole in, no hole to put the food or bone into and no material with which to cover it. A dog's food-hiding behaviour is an extremely instructive example of a series of instinctive actions which are completed once they have been released, and which in detail are not dependent on the situation containing adequate objects for the constituents of the activity.

Occasionally a dog learns that this activity can sometimes be carried out satisfactorily in a made-up bed, for instance, or on a sofa with cushions, but human beings are apt to oppose this. This activity leads to a satisfactory result as soon as the dog is no longer touching the bone with its nose. Purely anatomically, it would naturally be extremely easy for the dog to fetch material from another place if the covering fails. A number of dogs do fetch 'nest' material, such as blankets for its bed. But a dog doesn't move a thing with its teeth to cover a bone on a sofa. Fetching covering material thus seems to lie quite outside natural fixed patterns of behaviour. Out of doors, earth from some other place might possibly give the hiding place a smell alien to the surroundings, or a different appearance, which is perhaps the reason why dogs never cover bones with any material other than what lies at the edges of the hole. An action which would entail the transport of earth or other covering has therefore presumably not been able to develop.

The most stereotyped actions in hiding behaviour are evident in a number of features in a dog's way of reacting if it is disturbed in its burying activities. If you happen to come up to a dog whilst it is digging a hole or hiding a bone, it usually happens (if the dog has not unusually great confidence in you) that the dog takes the bone out of the hole again, goes a few yards to the side, but usually not out of sight, and buries the bone somewhere else. The same thing happens if another dog happens to see the burying, the result of which may be that the other dog later goes directly up to the place where the bone is hidden and digs it up.

Dogs have a disposition to guard bones they have buried, at least

E

for a few minutes, sometimes for several hours. They then lie with the head very near the covered bone, but with the nose pointing away from the place where the bone is hidden. They tend to stare at the hiding-place, and that the nose does not point towards the bone is considered to be because then it will not reveal the bone's position to other dogs, while in other situations a dog's nose does point straight at whatever it is that interests it.

With hackles raised and prepared to attack, the dachshund guards the hiding-place of its bone. Its gaze swings between the hiding-place and the approaching person. Next moment the dog will dig up the bone—or launch an attack.

Variations in bone-hiding behaviour hardly ever occur, except when associated with the tendency to move out of sight of people or of other dogs before the bone is hidden, or with how easily a dog can be made to dig up a bone and defend it. The degree of aggressiveness and familiarity with other dogs plays a considerable rôle here. My younger dachshund bitch never buries bones in sight of her mother, but the mother calmly buries bones in sight of her daughter. My first dachshund never buried bones in a person's sight and always hotly defended the area round her bone-hiding-place, usually within a radius of a few yards. She could then be very aggressive towards people too, although otherwise she was never inclined to resist members of the household. Broadly speaking, one can say that bone-hiding behaviour and associated aggressive behaviour show that dominant dogs clearly react less to the factors which in a subordinate dog lead to strong preparations for defence.

For several days, sometimes for weeks and even months, a dog can remember where it has buried a bone. Especially if in a playful mood, or if hungry, or also very often if another dog appears in the proximity of a hidden bone, a dog digs up bones which have been hidden for months and begins to gnaw them, or else it digs up the bone only to go and bury it again soon afterwards. It is evident that a special mood or another dog's sudden appearance near the hiding-place leads to the dog remembering where the bone is. The scent of the bone is certainly not decisive, as amongst other things the other dog would then react to the hiding-place.

A DOG'S CARE OF ITS BODY

Actions in wolves and dogs which serve the care of the body, or more indirectly concern it, are easy to recognise, but can occasionally appear in circumstances other than the functional sphere to which they really belong.

A dog which has got wet *shakes itself*. This same action, however, can appear as an anticipatory action in situations when there is certainly nothing which in any way would influence the body surface or coat. A dog also removes water from its coat by *licking,* primarily in this case its paws. Characteristic of a dog's shaking action is that the shaking cannot be carried out solely with the hind regions, solely with the tail or solely with the extremities. If a dog gets wet on its back or tail, then the water shaking movement begins with the head, or at least the shoulders. A cat—or any feline animal —can very elegantly shake one paw only. Dogs, on the other hand, can stop shaking, so that only the head and shoulders are shaken. Thus the shaking-wave need not reach, for instance, the tail.

A separate shaking of the head often occurs if a dog has some irritating infection in the aural passage. This shaking does not travel backwards, but is purely a head- and ear-shaking movement. It is often preceded by the dog holding its head on one side and its neck slightly downwards, which is not the introduction to removing water, for instance from its coat.

Other irritants besides a wet coat also release complete shaking movements. A dog that has been out in the cold in winter and comes into a warm stairwell shakes itself for a while. An alien object on a dog's back, inaccessible to the nose, releases shaking. The intention of shaking is that the dog stretches its neck slightly forward.

Shaking as an anticipatory action occurs when a dog suddenly receives some information which makes it highly expectant, especially if the expectation concerns something which entails increased activity—a walk, for instance. Sometimes shaking after sleep may be only a kind of body care. A dog rising from its bed often shakes itself when there is no question of any change of mood. But the more expectation a dog shows, the more certain it is that it will shake itself thoroughly as soon as it has risen from its bed or from the place where it was lying. One might possibly interpret this as a weak ritualisation of shaking behaviour. In any case, shaking in an expectant mood has the function of rousing other dogs' attention. If one of my dachshunds gets up from its bed and shakes itself strongly, this has a pronounced effect on the other one. Both dachshunds know that the other's shaking, if the action occurs with great intensity, means that something pleasant is going to happen. I do not know how dogs without experience react to other dogs' shaking ceremonies in expectant moods. Shaking alone is naturally not an activity which has a social function, but in combination with other elements in the behaviour complex of expectation, shaking has a signalling significance—if it has not this meaning from birth. Shaking combined with high-toned yawning is especially a sign of expectation.

A dog *scratches* its neck, chest, stomach and sides, using only its hindpaws. Parts not accessible to the hindpaws are accessible for de-lousing, i.e. swift chewing bites with the front teeth, often accompanied by licking. Scratching and de-lousing are released by light (tickling?) irritation of the skin. With its *forepaws,* a dog can *rub off* earth, for instance, from its nose and head, but the swift scraping movements of the kind it makes with its hindlegs cannot be carried out with the forelegs.

Irritation by or in the rectum release a special licking action; a dog *slides* along on its scutcheon, the function of which is probably the removal of tapeworms which have reached the rectal opening.

A dog's inclination to *eat grass* can be mentioned in this connection. It is very common that after a few hours a dog throws up the grass it has eaten and other stomach and intestinal contents come with it. Grass-eating can justifiably be called an activity primarily released by a state of indisposition due to an irritation of the stomach, but quite healthy dogs can also eat grass.

A dog which has been asleep or lain still for some time, *stretches* when it gets up. This activity is also less divided into separate elements than the corresponding activity in a cat. The stretching movements in a dog involve stretching its forelegs forwards and hindlegs backwards, at which the hindlegs may take incomplete steps, an amusing element in this action occurring occasionally when a dog travels forward, with both hindlegs dragging stretched out backwards. Stretching actions also entail a lowering and raising of the neck. Often a dog yawns at the end of stretching activity. Similar actions occur in all higher mammals, and their function is somewhat obscure. It has been said that they increase the circulation of the blood in muscles which have been relaxed for some time.

Many dogs *react to a clicking noise* in their coats. If you click your nails in a dog's coat and then show your fingers to the dog, it sniffs them and takes on an expression of both interest and displeasure. A dog does exactly the same when it sniffs at a tick, for instance, which it has bitten off itself. If you repeat the attempt, a dog reacts up to ten times to this sound. In wild dogs there are naturally several parasites, primarily lice and ticks, which burst with a click if a dog happens to catch them in its front teeth when it is de-lousing. Unfortunately lice are not all that rare in domestic dogs, even if in these days of modern insecticides they have become much less common than before. Dogs which have certainly never heard the sound of a louse or tick bursting also react to this noise, so the reaction is inborn.

Dogs lick *sores, rashes and injuries* which they have received. Veterinary surgeons are none too pleased at this behaviour in a dog, but in wild animals this form of care has obvious significance. By licking, a dog removes alien objects from the sore or injury, and often uses its teeth when doing so. Dogs which are very good friends tolerate one licking the other's injuries, as long as this does not involve pain. Dogs are inclined to investigate injuries to other dogs too, and to people. The slightest little scratch in a person's skin makes a dog sniff, sometimes retreat, and quite often the dog is inclined to want to lick a person's sores too. A dog reacts to fallen scabs etc. with the same expression as when it sniffs at a blood-filled tick.

Yawning has already been mentioned in connection with stretching movements. When a dog has just found out that something pleasant is to happen, it often yawns especially pronouncedly, and quite often lets out a long-drawn-out, usually rising sound. This type of yawning is obviously an anticipatory activity even more common than shaking movements. Naturally, a possible explanation of this might be that yawning could be a kind of preparation for increased physical activity, ventilation of the lungs being improved by deep breathing.

When a dog yawns as anticipatory activity to whoever happens to be there, it often opens its mouth over its master's hand. Why it does so is not known, but a possible explanation is that the opening of the mouth is so strongly linked with the sphere of function to which biting belongs that when opening its mouth the dog also carries out an action from the aggressive sphere of function—moving its jaws over an object which is just in front of its nose. A yawning dog never bites, however, at least not in association with yawning.

A dog's *nose-wiping movements* are meant to clean off food remnants from its lips. This action is inclined to develop into much more distinctive behaviour in which a dog lowers its foreparts and rubs the upper part of the head and throat on the ground. But this action can go even further: the dog rolls right over on to its back and wriggles both ways by twisting its spine. The whole of its back is then rubbed against the underlayer. This ceremony's introduction also often includes one or both forepaws several times rubbing from the eyes down over the nose.

Nose-wiping activity is seldom followed by vocalisations, but when it develops into back-rubbing, the dog often makes cooing or small growling sounds of quite different kinds, at the same time wagging its tail. A dog which carries out ordinary nose-wiping is contented, full and undisturbed. If the activity goes on into back-rubbing it is a sign that the dog is even more contented. When the dog gets up after the back-rubbing ceremony, it usually shakes itself, which is to put its coat in order.

In expectation of food, quite a lot of dogs carry out the back-rubbing ceremony direct, but not the introductory nose-wiping. This is released when the dog sees preparations for a meal, for instance, or when someone comes home with a packet of food, or when someone says 'Now I'll cook the dinner', or someone does something which the dog connects with the preparation of meals. I think that this behaviour can be explained in the following way: only a very contented and full dog carries out the back-rubbing ceremony, and a full dog is a contented dog. But a dog expecting a titbit in the near future is also a contented dog. So an association appears between contentment in different situations and back-rubbing behaviour, at which the back-rubbing ceremony also begins to be released in situations other than those associated with nose-wiping, presuming the dog is very contented. Finally on this point, contentment can also release back-rolling if the mood is not connected with food. But it must be said that this interpretation in purely instinctive terms may be faulty, for there can be other influential releasing factors which are not easy to establish.

A series of quick intensive scratches with the forepaws on some fairly soft underlayer, a rug, for instance, is sometimes the introduction to back-rubbing activity in anticipation of something not associated with food. Perhaps the origin of this movement lies in the rubbing of the nose with the paws, but as in this situation the nose does not need wiping, it passes into another activity. Other dogs, however, behave differently, and small, short leaps and play actions can also occur in this situation.

For many domestic dogs, back-rubbing behaviour and wiping the nose takes on the character, naturally quite unconsciously, of thanks-for-the-food-ceremony, or soon-there-will-be-food-ceremony, and sometimes the ceremony means just-think-how-nice-it-will-be. Back-rubbing and nose-wiping occur on a softish, preferably rough underlayer. Rugs are often the ideal place for this behaviour. But nose-wiping can be carried out against objects at nose-height. My Scottie sometimes wipes his nose, which is whiskery and thoroughly messed-up with food remnants, on outer clothing hanging in the closet.

Related to genuine nose-wiping after a meal is *nose-rubbing against wet new snow*. This behaviour is not common to all dogs. The three Scottish terriers which I have known often did this if the opportunity arose, but only if one of my three dachshunds had shown inclinations to the same behaviour. The action is a thoroughly carried out nose-cleaning, in which the dog, with the help of its hindlegs, pushes itself forwards several yards on its chest, holding its forelegs passively stretched backwards, and alternately thrusts first one then the other side of its nose against the snow.

Closely related to nose-wiping and back-rubbing behaviour, but released by other stimuli, is a dog's habit of *rolling in (what to us is a malodorous) substratum* of varying origins, an unpleasant habit, to say the least. The scent, not the structure of the substratum, is decisive. My dachshunds, like all other good clean domestic dogs, have rolled in excrement of very different kinds, in decayed fish, in the remains of mammal carcasses of varying consistency, such as vole-corpses and seals that have been dead for some years, and in decayed dried-up birds killed by oil. They also roll on ground in which the scent of the above remains. When rolling like this, a dog does not wag its tail, and the rolling is not so pronounced as the back-rubbing mentioned above in thanks and anticipation ceremonies. The sides of the neck become especially affected.

There is no definite explanation for this behaviour. It has been suggested that in this artificial way the dog changes its own scent, either to make it less identifiable or to make its presence more obvious. But despite its indefinite ethological function, it has a very strong motivation and it is difficult to get dogs to stop this habit. They go on rolling even if they know that this behaviour is followed by immediate punishment, for instance in the form of a very unpleasant cold bath.

With an expression of pleasure, a dog rolls in matter which to humans is unpleasant and malodorous.

Dogs never wash themselves. When a dog wades out into water, it is because the dog is too warm or is seeking some object in the water, not trying to get clean. Many dogs like going into water and even swim quite voluntarily sometimes. But this behaviour is clearly an activity from the hunting sphere of function or one with which the dog cools itself. Some dogs' dislike of being washed and scrubbed often leads them to behave afterwards in a way that indicates a hidden aggressive mood that has existed throughout the washing procedure. For example, after a bath, a dog may take hold of the towel and then play in a manner which shows clear signs of aggression. The violence of the movements and noisy vocalisations also indicate that the apparent playfulness is not simply play.

A dog's way of placing *excrement and urine* is primarily connected with territorial-marking behaviour and hence with social behaviour.

In connection with the care of the body, it only need be pointed out that healthy adult dogs never soil with their urine the places where they usually are. On the other hand quite healthy dogs, especially in association with false pregnancy and whelping, may urinate in places which from a human point of view are unsuitable. The background to this urinating is strong motivation of some kind and punishment has no effect. Often at the moment of taking such action, a dog is frightened of punishment, but it urinates all the same.

SOCIAL RELATIONS

Dominance and subordinance

In a wolf-pack, or in a team of dogs, and in most situations in which two dogs live together, it is usual that an individual rises to the dominant position. This rank order is not necessarily expressed in daily life, but on the other hand it is even more marked in special situations.

For part of the year, a wolf is essentially a pack-animal. For the other part of the year, it either lives a fairly pronounced domestic life or a solitary life. This naturally entails that instinctive behaviour patterns in a wolf must be adapted to both pack-life and domestic life as well as solitary life. Catching of prey of many different kinds also makes great demands on a wolf's innate behaviour, and also at the same time on its ability to learn. The golden jackal, as well as the dingo and pariah dog, both of which are usually designated descendants of domestic dogs, though are considered by some researchers to be the progenitors of dogs, live a pack life as well as domestic and solitary life. The opinions that follow are thus valid, even if the wolf could not be the progenitor of the dog.

The rank order between individuals can thus be decided in very different ways, both in dogs and wolves. Sometimes it is a result of harsh battles, sometimes a clear rank order appears quite without apparent disputes, but usually it is a result of displays of different kinds. Anyhow, when it concerns dogs, the rank order is decided in most cases without fighting. Open contests of strength between dogs which are not especially aggressive occur primarily in connection with male dogs competing for a bitch in season. Relations between dogs which know each other are on the other hand usually the result of displays of varying degrees of strength. Social rank order can thus be the result of confrontations in which it is hard to distinguish between play and brief momentary outbreaks of weak aggression. During such series of actions, dogs often make clear and lifelong ties of friendship, although at the same time these lead to a rank order between individuals being defined. Such a friendship, however, is often expressed by the dogs ignoring one another, or that when they do meet by chance, then there is much happy tail-wagging and a few seconds' sniffing, and then they go off in different directions. This friendship can also lead to dogs playing very intensively or hunting together when they meet.

The result of actions which without real conflicts lead to a certain rank order between two or more dogs is usually the same as if the dogs had arranged their relationships through direct conflict. At the same time, bitches and pups release social inhibitions which enable most bitches to obtain a rank higher than equally strong and even stronger male dogs. In some special cases, however, the dominant position in a pack of dogs may be so sought after that it can lead to open warfare. Descriptions of sledge-dog fights for dominance a team are certainly not simply imagination. The very fact that the dominant dog has to run first in a team may be a sought-after advantage.

Dogs in our circumstances are not such pronounced pack-animals as wolves in the winter. For one thing, we do not really keep dogs in packs, and also it seems that domestication has lessened the strength of pack-forming behaviour. Most dogs are intended, anyhow in hunting, shepherding and guarding, etc., for working alone or at the most a few together, so strong inclinations to pack-formation have not had any selection advantage, at least not in the recent history of dog-breeding. In addition, a bitch's quick sexual cycle (two seasons as against one per year in a wolf) and quick sexual maturing (usually under a year, as against two to three years in a wolf) have resulted in the dog's yearly cycle and life having less room for social life than a wolf's. But despite this, a dog retains all the behaviour patterns which a wolf uses in its social relationships.

The individual in a pack which stands highest in the rank order is said to dominate the other members of the pack. The ethological terms *dominance* and *dominant* mean quite simply the opposite of inferiority, subordinate position, in fact weakness. The individual which is next highest in rank is dominant over all others except the strongest, and so on, though with some exceptions which will be dealt with below. For adult dogs with normal temperaments, the following highly natural rules on social dominance prevail. A large dog dominates over a small dog. A strong dog dominates over a weak dog. A fully developed dog dominates over young immature dogs of about the same strength. A bitch dominates over a male dog. These are, however, only basic rules, and the exceptions are in reality very numerous. A dog's temperament—bad temper, roughness, playfulness, pack-formation tendency, cowardice, timidity, etc.—is often of much greater significance than its size. It can happen that a young dog without experience of how serious a conflict can be, rises to a rank higher than its strength allows, only because an older and stronger dog may be disinclined through aggressive behaviour to keep a foreign and seldom-seen neighbour in check.

Modern investigations into rank orders in dog packs, primarily in litters of growing pups and young dogs which have been isolated, show that the rank order does not have to be linear. Usually one dog in such a pack is clearly dominant over all the others, and also a certain individual is usually an obvious scapegoat, which all the other members of the pack tyrannise. In the middle categories, it is not unknown that chance is decisive for how the rank order is stabilised. The rank order in a pack of dogs can be A–B–C–D–E–F, but at the same time dog E can, for instance, be clearly dominant over dog C. The result in this case becomes a rank order triangle

CDEC. A rank order is very inclined to remain for a long time, just as it once happened to become established. It demands infusion of quite new factors for an established rank order to be broken up before a member is put out of the running for age reasons.

The social rank order of dogs can be influenced by the attitude of the owner towards a dog's behaviour and also by the mood of the owner. Thus it is often the owner who indirectly decides which rank a good-tempered dog takes in relation to other dogs roughly equal in size, which the dog often meets on daily walks, for instance. One of my dachshunds does not like walking through a certain park (rough stuff!) if no one but her master is with her, but if both her master and mistress are there, she is not at all afraid. The slightest sense of reluctance in the person walking a dog can influence the mood of a sensitive and uncertain dog and with that also its inclination to vindicate itself at eventual confrontations with other dogs. A dog which receives support from its master becomes considerably more confident in its behaviour, at least towards strange dogs. It can then rise into a higher place in the rank order than its strength and sex presupposes. If on the other hand its owner is negatively disposed to rough behaviour in a dog when it is confronted with other dogs, the dog's rank easily becomes lower than its strength, sex and temperament should allow. This primarily concerns smaller dogs, but larger dogs, if they are not of a rough disposition, are also influenced by human moods.

A dog which is dominant in relation to a dog it meets behaves with great confidence, and this is easy to see. But it can happen that a dominant dog gives the impression of ignoring subordinate dogs it meets, in a most obvious manner. This ignoring is in itself a sign of a complete absence of fear. Subordinate dogs never ignore dogs they meet which they know stand higher than themselves in the rank order. A subordinate dog often looks away from a dominant dog. Looking away, or turning the whole head right away, is clearly a so-called appeasement gesture with which the subordinate dog automatically shows its inferiority, and which in strong dogs inhibits the carrying through of an attack.

Dogs which are rough by nature, and which are usually kept on a lead, are difficult to get to accept each other. This is often one of a dog-owner's troubles. Acceptance should preferably not occur in such a way that the dogs first fall out with each other. A fight between two dogs on leads does not solve the rank order problem; on the contrary this may well complicate matters. And if one dog is on a lead and the other free, the situation becomes especially provocative. Most dogs, however, are so constituted that there is no fighting over rank order if they are allowed to run free. If the differences in body-strength and size are great, the situation is often solved by this alone, for the weaker knows it is subordinate. But if the smaller dog has a very fiery temperament, then size is not a decisive factor.

The ceremonies which a dog carries out when it meets a strange dog, and which determine its relations to the stranger at any eventual meeting, are of basic significance because of this effect in the future. It can be repeated that dogs which do not compete over their food with another dog, or for man's favour, do not need to decide actively which is the physically stronger. And a dog does not do this if it is of normal disposition and if its owner does not influence it. An influence, however, can occur quite unconsciously, and the decision to keep a dog of high rank on a lead often makes it very difficult to achieve natural relations between those dogs which, during their daily walks for instance, see each other, but are not allowed to run around freely.

It is already evident that a dog has special actions which in conflict-situations lessen the risk of fights and which in fights stop dogs seriously injuring each other. These appeasement gestures are a presupposition for the rank order and pack systems which wolves and dogs show. If all rank order or other disputes ended in open warfare, then fights would be very common and would lead to numerous casualties. In actual fact, most dog conflicts, however serious they may sound, are almost totally bloodless, and minor scratches are the only injuries dogs usually inflict on each other. The fight quickly results in some appeasement gesture by the subordinate dog, at which the threatening situation gradually dissolves with neither dog seriously injuring the other. Some individuals, however, are inclined to attack at once all dogs which they think they can win over. This behaviour is abnormal, and faults in early training may be the main reason.

A dispute between two dogs often develops according to the following schedule—presuming that the dogs can move about fairly freely and the owners do not influence the dogs' behaviour in any way at all. As the dogs approach each other, they begin to walk 'stiff-leggedly', in other words they take up display postures. Their hackles often rise, at least slightly, and the position of their tails and ears also shows preparation for a fight. If very aggressive dogs are involved, they may also growl. With great caution the dogs investigate the scents around each other's hindquarters. If the dogs are of different sexes, then the male dog especially usually begins to wag its tail and simultaneously also show other signs that its aggressiveness is disappearing. A bitch, on the other hand, may go on moving in a display posture, but with fewer aggressive signs. The opponent has clearly shown by its friendliness that it has no aggressive intentions and at the same time has also demonstrated its inferiority in the rank order.

This same peaceful conclusion usually arises with dogs of the same sex, despite the threatening introduction. Tails begin to wag, at least one of them, at first insignificantly and high up, then more clearly and somewhat lower down. If two male dogs are involved, then perhaps each walks to a different lamp-post and leaves a 'visiting card', at which they fairly calmly go off in different directions and in a more subdued display posture. But sometimes it is different: display behaviour becomes more and more evident, growls louder, lips curling, baring the fangs facing the opponent, and suddenly the situation explodes into a fight. The one that is weaker or fails in its attempts to get a grip anywhere, or is crowded by the other, may however suddenly show an appeasement gesture in the middle of the fight, which inhibits its opponent's biting, however angry it may be. This very important appeasement gesture takes the form of the crowded dog suddenly lowering its head a little and holding it turned away from the stronger dog. In this way the weaker one exposes its neck or its shoulder region to its opponent, and then the stronger cannot bring itself to bite, however simple that would be. The growling goes on and the aggressive mood persists, but the fight is interrupted as long as the subordinate dog shows an appeasement gesture. Sometimes the subordinate

Extreme aggressive mood with simultaneous strong social inhibition against attack. Each dog has turned its vulnerable neck towards and its head away from its opponent.

dog in this situation may then flee, but it can also happen that the fight flares up again. The result then is usually that the subordinate dog soon has to take up an appeasement posture again. The stronger may then continue growling and may even make intentions to bite, but it cannot inflict any serious injuries as long as its opponent holds out its throat and turns away its head. It often happens at this stage of the fight that the dominant dog jumps up against its opponent and places its paws on the back or neck. The subordinate dog usually does not dare engage with any great strength against this pronounced demonstration of power, so just growls and holds its tail erect.

If the dogs are on leads and not free to approach each other, however, the risk of direct aggression and injuries becomes much greater. A dog's reaction to something towards which it is aggressive and at the same time a little afraid of, is to bark, which would be released very easily if the dog were on a lead. As soon as one dog begins to bark, then the other begins, intensively and angrily, growling at the same time, their hackles rising, and also perhaps baring their teeth. It needs only a couple of confrontations of this kind for two dogs to regard each other for ever as some kind of hereditary enemy, at least as long as they do not meet except when on a lead. If they meet later when free, it would very easily immediately lead to a real fight, which naturally becomes intensive because neither dog has had any experience which would 'tell' it that the other is dangerous. So dogs should, even if they are on a lead, be allowed to get to know other dogs which they will often see on their daily walks. This introduction need not be combined with any conclusive acquaintance. A dog which is otherwise inclined to be aggressive can be directed with a light hand to 'acquaintance-making-sniffing', to become either reasonably indifferent or even very friendly towards most other dogs round about. It is a question of ensuring that neither dog has the opportunity of showing obvious aggression when they first meet, and it is also necessary that the dogs are allowed in the customary dog-manner to sniff each other. If this ceremony is not allowed to occur, it may happen that the atmosphere remains tense. It is easiest to allow the dogs to accept each other if the newcomer is introduced as a pup to the older dogs in the area.

Variations of the above-mentioned appeasement behaviour also occur in conflicts of another type. My dachshunds give good examples of this, especially in the conflict which regularly occurs when the mother pushes her much lighter daughter away from her food-bowl. The subordinate bitch cannot bite her mother, who is standing with her head in the subordinate one's food-bowl, bent

F

over and with her throat quite open to bite. But as long as the mother holds her head like this, the daughter does everything she can to bite the mother's ears and nose. Another variation also occurs. The subordinate one stands with her head and neck above the mother's neck, but holding her head turned away, and growling in a terrifying manner.

There are transitions between aggressive-appeasement and the measures associated with humble subordination, i.e. lowering the fore-regions, tail-wagging at low level or between the legs, ears back, the position of the corners of the mouth, rolling over on the back. But the speed with which dogs move in a fight, jump up and bite at each other, makes it very difficult to see details in behaviour and consider how actions pass into each other. In real fighting appeasement, both the dogs involved, the subordinate one too, hold their tails fairly strongly erect and their muscles tense.

An aggressive situation has a long aftermath. My dachshunds do not become friends again for some hours after a dispute over food-bowls, which means the dominant one would probably be friendly, but the subordinate one growls and is upset as soon as the mother comes near her. Not until the following day is the conflict forgotten. Repeated confrontations with the mother when the latter is no longer aggressive make the daughter return to normal friendship with the mother. If, on the other hand, two dogs which are not constantly in each other's presence set about each other and do not complete the fight so that the one becomes definitely placed lower in the rank order, then the inclination to take up this contest of strength at the first opportunity remains for years, perhaps for the whole of the dog's life. So it is important to allow dogs to get to know each other in a way that does not release direct aggression.

A dog which is superior to its opponent can acquire extreme respect by gripping its opponent by the scruff of the neck and shaking it. This presupposes, of course, considerable difference in sizes. A dog cannot lift an equally large dog by the scruff of the neck. Even man can acquire respect in a dog in the same way, but this action is not likely to give the dog great confidence in its master. It is a demonstration of power which should not be used thoughtlessly, as it can lead to timidity in the dog.

A dominant dog need by no means display its superiority. It can be said perhaps that a dog which is able to quell an opponent, if necessary, does not bother to do so as long as the opponent does not behave challengingly, and sometimes the opponent may even behave in quite an impudent way without the stronger dog bothering about it. The dominant dog is not really being exposed to any real disrespect, and can do what it wants without the subordinate dog stopping it.

It often happens that an older dog which in general is not so easy to stimulate into various actions prefers to take a roundabout route instead of being forced to inspire respect in smaller and weaker dogs through display behaviour. For instance, it makes it quite clear to the person leading it that it wishes to cross to the opposite pavement. But if despite everything a confrontation cannot be avoided, it demonstrates its superiority effectively. Not until a dog has reached a really great age, i.e. shows marked symptoms of age, does it step aside in the struggle for rank order and give up its position. Old dogs' disinclination to take up the fight results in that they are quite often allowed to retain their rank throughout their lives among the dogs they know.

Bitches usually dominate over male dogs, irrespective of the size of the male dog. This can lead to a docile male dog, which lives in the same home as a bad-tempered bitch, not daring to take the initiative of mating with the bitch, and sometimes not even daring to react to the bitch's mating invitations. This kind of dog is so strongly adjusted to the bitch being aggressive that it cannot overcome its fear of her. On the other hand, for strange bitches, which have not had the opportunity to confirm their position through repeated aggressiveness, the same male dog has no respect which would stop it making urgent approaches, even against the bitch's will.

Normal dogs, irrespective of sex, react only slightly aggressively if a pup or an immature young dog happens to behave impudently towards them. Thus dogs have strong social inhibitions towards pups and young dogs which stop the pups and young dogs finding themselves in conflicts with older, stronger dogs. Most pups and young dogs are usually extremely friendly in their behaviour towards older dogs and strongly disposed to demonstrate their subordination with very definite appeasement behaviour. There are, however, both abnormal young dogs and abnormally reacting older dogs, with which confrontations with adult dogs or pups respectively can end in disastrous results. A young dog which really attacks, naturally often (but not always) releases full aggression in adult dogs, irrespective of sex. There are also some older dogs of this kind which unhesitatingly snap at pups so that they can incur serious injuries. So a certain caution is necessary when one is walking a pup, but at the same time it should be remembered that it is important that pups and young dogs are allowed in a normal way to get to know the dogs which they will later be meeting very often.

Many totally normal adult dogs react with a certain annoyance to a happy, playful pup's intensive play invitations. But a brief growl and a light snapping bite, though without any sign of direct anger, forces the pup to keep away. A pup who experiences this will probably remain all its life subordinate in rank order to any dog which rejects it in this way, if no provocative situation arises at any time leading to a total re-evaluation. A large dog can continue to be very humble towards a small but older dog, irrespective of the sex of the two dogs. If, however, these dogs should live together for the rest of their lives, dominance would gradually be decided from outside the real situation concerning strength and sex, and not on the basis of 'childhood experience'. This happens, for instance, in a wolf pack and in dog kennels. But most domestic dogs are confronted sufficiently seldom with other dogs in the same area that relations which were stabilised on the basis of pup experiences easily become lasting.

Having read these descriptions of situations in which dogs may or should come into conflict with each other and in which dominance-relations develop, there are perhaps some readers who may wonder whether it is really so that dogs which live together are constantly in a state of some kind of tension. This is, however, not the case. Dominance and subordinance are actualised only in conflict and competitive situations. In wild wolves, members of the pack can for a long time avoid every situation of the kind that rank order would actualise. They can in fact appear to live wholly without rank order, at least if sexual competitive circumstances do not intrude. But in wolves which are enclosed in a small space in a zoo, the rank order is actualised between members time and time again. They cannot, for example, unnoticeably avoid each other, which is necessary if aggressive behaviour is not to be released in the stronger ones at meeting.

In the comfortable life that most domestic and sporting dogs lead, social dominance in everyday life plays a rather insignificant rôle. But in wild animals, in a pack of wolves for instance, the rank order system is one of the mechanisms which in times of food shortage can lead first to the less useful members being eliminated. The strongest and most experienced get the most food and therefore also opportunities to survive during periods of food-shortage. But at the same time, it can happen that a very hungry animal may fight itself up to a better place than its normal rank would assume, through strong aggressiveness for short periods, and an animal which has already eaten is momentarily not so inclined to defend its position in the rank order scale. This also occurs in dogs.

The following features of my two bitches' behaviour give some insight into how dominance relations influence two dogs well known to each other. Both dachshunds often sleep in the same bed, but they have never been able to eat simultaneously out of the same food-bowl, which, on the other hand, my Scottish terrier bitch and her adult daughter could easily do without conflict. The stronger dachshund bitch, the mother, also drives her daughter away with brutal violence from her food-bowl, as soon as the mother has finished her share of the food. Because of her size, the mother eats rather more quickly than the daughter. As she gobbles her own food, she carefully keeps an eye on how far her daughter has got with her share. When after a while there is clearly more left in the daughter's bowl than in the mother's, the mother throws herself at her daughter and eats up the rest of her share, while the daughter, howling, but inhibited from attacking, stands aside. The mother may even then run back to her own bowl and finish off her own food. At this stage the daughter is so upset that she does not react to the other bowl. And yet she is not afraid to do that. Badly brought-up dogs! A correct comment, but just because they are badly brought up, it has been possible to make this behavioural analysis. In a 'natural' situation the daughter would move away with her food (prey, a piece of meat, etc.). In this way, a large number of conflicts are avoided in wolf-packs, for instance, which otherwise would threaten. Larger prey, of course, naturally give more animals a chance to eat at the same time, so the situation with the two food-bowls is a very artificial one.

Between meals there rarely seems to be any clear rank order between these two dachshunds. It may happen that the younger one is forced to make way for the older one, in a much favoured corner, for instance, though she is not directly driven away, but the older one lies down and gradually pushes the younger one off the favoured spot. On walks, the younger one regularly places her 'visiting card' on or beside the older one's. The rank order between the two bitches is most clearly expressed in ordinary life by the younger one following much more carefully what the older one is doing, than the older one following what the younger one is up to. If, especially, the older one is anxious about something, then the younger one becomes very worried and frightened, whilst the older one takes only little interest in what the younger one eventually begins to react to. In these dogs, the older's dominance is expressed primarily in that the younger one in her relations to the mother has remained on a level which quite often reminds me of a not-yet-adult young dog—at the time of writing, she is eight years old, and the mother ten. So it is not just in human relations that an individual, subordinate in temperament and harshness, can remain completely dominated by a powerful mother far into middle age. Finally, it can be mentioned that when playing the older dachshund easily becomes slightly aggressive towards the younger, and an obvious rivalry for the favours of the members of the household exists.

Greeting behaviour

A dog's greeting behaviour is a demonstration of its friendly mood. Neither is there any doubt that a dog really does experience something much like our joy when it is in the mood which causes greeting activity. After the greeting itself, a dog still remains in a clearly happy and contented mood. As long as this mood prevails, a dog tries to stay close to the person who released the greeting behaviour. A dog, for example, likes to sit on the lap of a person who has been away a long time.

The most important greeting action is the previously mentioned tail-wagging. But added to this are a number of other actions which have their original or main function in quite different circumstances, but which to a very great extent leave an impression on a dog which is greeting intensively. Most dogs lick (or want to lick) the people they are greeting. This action may originate from begging for food in older wolf-cubs. Wolf-cubs lick their parents' lip regions, and in this way release regurgitation of food. A dog's greeting licks are directed primarily towards a person's mouth, and not until a dog is forbidden to lick the mouth and nose does it direct the licking towards the hands, for instance. Licking as greeting behaviour can be interpreted as evidence that a dog, in certain aspects of its relations to humans, is on the development and dependence level of an older wolf-cub.

It is very common for a dog, when it hears its name called or in some other way is addressed in friendly tones, to react with a licking intention, an intention to lick as with greeting.

Included in greeting behaviour is often whole series of anticipatory actions, which can be vocalisations, play actions and actions which belong within spheres of function with aggressive content. Among the actions included in the last type, the baring of teeth ('laughing') is the most common. Generally, however, anticipatory actions indicating non-aggressive playful moods are most common in greeting. One can perhaps say that a dog in general chooses from several different anticipatory actions or behaviour those which belong to the type of mood which is close to the greeting's joyful mood. Appeals to play thus belong to the most common activities in greeting mood.

Territory-marking

The marking of territory occurs in canines either with urine or excrement, or with both, and neither wolves nor dogs are exceptions to this rule. They mark their territories with both urine and excrement, but with most emphasis on urine-marking. A dog, however, has well-developed anal-glands which give its excrement an individual scent. A surplus of fluid in these glands sometimes gives a dog briefly a strong smell of anchovies, which infallibly releases an intensive licking of the anal region to remove the scent. Beyond its direct function in territory-marking, urinating is important as a pure display action. A male dog urinates when it meets almost any strange dog, regardless of its sex. The more a male dog's urinating has the character of display action, the higher the dog places its scent-marking. If the urination is only carried out to empty the bladder, after a too long spell indoors for instance, then it may happen that a male dog doesn't cock its leg and urinates without choosing a place. It then stands with its feet apart, its hindlegs well back and hind regions lowered. It is cruelty to animals to walk a dog so seldom that it urinates in this way! In normal cases, a male dog urinates in small, then very small spurts, so if an unexpected display situation arises towards the end of the walk, a dog is still usually able to manage a few drops against a tree or some other suitable, or indeed unsuitable, object.

A male dog's choice of place for urinating is normally decided primarily by the scent world of the territory. A dog which is regularly walked through territory where other male dogs are walked, seeks out as many of the other dogs' scent-markings as possible and tries to cover them. A dog recognises scent-markings which the territory's other dogs have made. The scent-marking alone makes a dog aggressive, if the dog who has left it is an 'enemy'. Dogs which are good friends, on the other hand, do not react much to each other's markings, both in relations between bitches and relations between male dogs. It has sometimes been maintained that dogs are able to establish from the height of the marking whether a male dog who has made the marking is 'dangerous'. Naturally it may be that among equal-sized dogs, the male dog which happens to be the most disposed to display on an average always marks highest. But the marking does not occur with such great precision that it would be easy for other dogs to interpret this scent-mark's mood-content in detail. A dog stems from the wolf, which has nowhere near such a variation in size as the dog, with its many breeds, so it is highly unlikely that a dog could use the height of a marking as a sign of how dangerous the dog that had made it might be. A small dog may regard a large dog as its friend, but has real enemies among the territory's smallest dogs.

Bitches thoroughly inspect male dogs' markings, but do not usually place their urine on a male dog's. It is very difficult to fathom all the different factors which decide where a bitch urinates. She seeks out a place with much greater care than a male dog, if the circumstances are such that she can peacefully devote herself to this innate behaviour. Often the urine is placed close to some male dog's scent-mark. The main impression one gets is that the placing is done so that the male dog can easily find the marking, but that the marking should not be covered by male dogs' incessantly repeated markings on posts, etc., round about. In extreme cold, or in rain, or if the bitch is very much taken up by some preparation, for a hunting trip, for instance, she urinates clearly only so that it shall quickly be over, without choosing a place at all, even if the need to

urinate is not great. In special situations she also learns to urinate to
order on an indicated place. On the other hand, male dogs can in
such cases seldom overcome the impulse to seek out some suitable
place for their scent-markings.

Just as male dogs cover up other male dogs' markings, so does a
bitch very often place her urine on or just beside other bitches'
urine. If you take two bitches out for a walk, the dominant one
usually urinates first, and then the subordinate one places her
scent-marking on the dominant one's or just beside it. This is also
so among male dogs when they meet each other; the dominant one
urinates first and the weaker one afterwards, if the opportunity
arises to attempt to cover the marking as far as is possible.

Dogs on a visit in strange homes sometimes have a strong
inclination to leave a urine 'visiting-card' behind them. Male dogs
on a visit in homes where there is a bitch do this very easily. On
later visits, they then go to the 'visiting card' place and investigate
to see if it has been covered by another dog. Male dogs are especially inclined to do this if there is a bitch in season in the house. The
visit may well strain human relations—so in these circumstances
leave your male dog at home if it has no mission to accomplish!
Bitches, too, on a visit to a strange house may leave their visiting
cards behind them, and this can happen even in houses where there
is no dog at all. Punishment is no use against this behaviour. A
bitch which has this tendency attempts to make her marking even if
it is quite clear that it is forbidden. My first dachshund bitch had a
habit of placing a few drops on the hall mat at the end of a visit.
But this behaviour is much rarer in bitches than in male dogs.

Some bitches, during the long periods when they are sexually
inactive, may show covering behaviour which is approximate to a
male dog's. They may even lift one hindleg slightly when they
urinate and they sometimes urinate in smaller portions than
normally. In all bitches, however, interest in male dogs' markings is
greatest just before they come into season or during the first few
days. During this time, a bitch normally often has a very clear
tendency to divide up her urinating into many portions, in that way

marking her presence and her physiological condition for the male dogs in the area.

Dogs usually place their excrement to one side of paths they generally use themselves. What the significance of this is is not known for certain. Carolus Linnaeus says in his short though in many ways extremely acute book on dogs, that a dog preferably places its excrement on some insignificant elevation. In Linnaeus' day hardly any dogs were kept on a lead, so one can presume that the choice of place then was not noticeably influenced by where man might wish his dog to open its bowels. Nowadays, however, it is often hard to trace any tendency to place excrement on elevations, but the fox has a strong inclination to place its excrement on stones, for instance. The anal glands give dogs' excrement an individual scent, which makes the excrement very suitable for territorial marking.

The actual choosing of a place is done with very great care in a dog. But it is difficult to understand which scents are then decisive. The place is chosen just as carefully, even if no other dog has visited the place for perhaps years. I think that when searching for a place for its excrement, a dog, strives to accomplish this on a place where it already finds its own scent. A dog completes its toilet more quickly if you do not let it walk on while it is seeking a place. Then it willingly walks back, largely in its own tracks, turns and goes back and forth across the tracks and then decides on a place.

Dogs of both sexes *scratch with both forelegs and hindlegs* after opening their bowels. A number of dogs also do this after marking with urine in association with pronounced display. This action never results in the excrement or the urine being covered over. It is thought that this behaviour may increase the spread of the scent and thus make the marking more effective. This explanation, however, is a little forced. This behaviour often occurs quite pronouncedly, irrespective of whether other dogs are around, and also in places where no other dogs have been for a very long time, even several years. In general, an alert observer can see from his dog whether after opening its bowels it will scratch with its legs or not.

If the dog is activated and content, or if it is in a display mood, then it makes the scratching movements, otherwise it usually does not. In addition, different individuals vary a great deal when it comes to this action's intensity and occurrence. My male Scottie only scratched after urinating if other male dogs were nearby, but sometimes after opening its bowels irrespective of other dogs, though far from after every bowel-opening. My dachshund bitches scratch only if they are excited in some way, but only very seldom after urinating.

SEXUAL RELATIONS

Twice a year a bitch comes into season, while the male dog can mate all the year round. A bitch's sexual cycle is thus different from a wolf's which has a season only once a year. There are, however, bitches which have a longer pause between seasons.

A bitch's behaviour changes markedly before she comes into season. The first sign that her season is approaching is often that she is inclined to divide up her urinating into smaller portions, and that she shows great care in her choice of place for urinating. One might say that it passes from mild marking-urinating into a pronounced marking. Through this behaviour the bitch spreads the knowledge of her coming season within the whole territory in which she usually resides, or where she is exercised. Different bitches, however, vary quite a lot in this respect. My older dachshund, which is a pronounced female type, shows very pronounced marking behaviour before and during her season. The younger dachshund, which during periods between seasons is pronouncedly sexless for a long time, both outwardly and in disposition, is on the other hand not nearly so inclined to proclaim her coming state, but during her actual season her marking behaviour gradually grows more pronounced. A number of bitches show a marked disquiet and an increasing wish to be taken for a walk when they are coming into season.

As a bitch comes into season, male dogs are at first only fairly interested, but towards the middle and end of the period their importunity is often incredible. It can happen that male dogs hang about the home of a bitch in season for days and days, without eating or going home. As long as the bitch is not out, male dogs paying attendance on the same bitch may remain reasonably neutral towards each other, but as soon as the bitch is present, the rank order between the males is at once relevant. But the bitch does not choose her favourite according to the males' rank order.

A bitch's mating invitation could hardly be misunderstood!
Dogs have no breed-inhibitions, but difference in size may be a hindrance.

Dogs that she has known before, or of which she is not afraid and which even in normal circumstances are not aggressive towards her, have the greatest chance of quickly winning her favour. A smaller bitch is usually rather afraid of too aggressive, or harsh, or large males which she does not know, even if, especially during her season, they usually stand highest in rank order among most male dogs. But it is by no means inevitable that a bitch accepts, from a human judgement point of view, the courtship of a suitable male, and instead she may well direct her invitations to some other dog.

Her attendant's 'handsomeness' (according to human values, purity of breed) is of no importance whatsoever, nor his breed, but his manner, the bitch's previous experience of different breeds and the environment in which her attendant appears, seem to be significant. Without the isolation which humans keep between different breeds, dogs would mate quite irrespective of breed, as long as the difference in sizes allowed it. During the season's first eight to ten days, a bitch does not invite males to mate, and neither does she accept any eventual approaches from the male. Towards the end of the period, her willingness to mate increases very markedly, and simultaneously the male's interest in the bitch increases correspondingly. A bitch can invite mating up to twenty days after the beginning of her season, and conception can even then still be the result.

Genuine invitations to mate in a bitch are extremely clear, and one might even say that they are 'challenging'. She stands with her neck lowered and head slightly turned away, her forefeet far apart and ears laid back (subordinance expression!) close to the male, her hindquarters often even directly touching the male's shoulder region. If the male does not react sufficiently to start mating, a bitch stands for a few seconds in an ordinary position, but then repeats her invitation posture, often even more pronouncedly. Her tail is sharply turned away, or if it is normally erect, bent slightly sideways across her back. The whole area round her genital opening is raised and demonstrated emphatically. Appeasement components in her behaviour are at the same time very pronounced and naturally cause the male, who is normally subordinate to the bitch in rank and especially subordinate to a bitch in season, to dare to approach her. A bitch's mating invitation may be introduced with play appeals.

Some bitches in season are actively inclined to seek out males, and others show no particular interest in males other than at the actual invitation to mating. I have found no difference in behaviour towards other bitches in my own bitches. A trace of lessening friendship towards people, on the other hand, continues almost throughout the season. Bitches which have strong appetitive behaviour for sexual activity naturally devote less time when in season to other behaviour than they normally would. There are bitches whose behaviour when in season is so totally directed at meeting males that even eating and sleeping are neglected. The bitch whines and begs to be let out for most of the day, especially if she can hear or scent her attendant males. In most bitches, however, behaviour deviates very little from the normal, other than when they happen to meet a male dog.

A male dog's first reaction when it meets a bitch in season is to demonstrate benevolence. Simultaneously, he attempts to demonstrate his right of ownership to a territory, i.e. he makes repeated urine-markings near the bitch, returning for a few moments to the bitch between markings. Individual variations in males, however, are very great, and experience and age are considered to play a certain rôle. It is easier mating an experienced male with an inexperienced bitch than mating two dogs which have no experience at all. To what extent this is a question of purely technically greater ability, or whether an older dog perhaps shows a more mature and therefore more efficient pattern of instinctive actions, is not known. An older dog, however, can be presumed to act more purposefully, if only because it is not distracted so much by irrelevancies. An experienced male is, for instance, not so frightened of the bitch when it has had previous experiences of this kind. It is usual that males invite bitches in season to play, and lick or try to lick the bitch's nose, ears, and genital region, and they do not defend themselves at all if the bitch becomes aggressive. It is extremely rare that male dogs are aggressive towards bitches, while bitches in season on the other hand are quite often, and may reject quite sharply a number of males, but then immediately afterwards invite others to mount her. Bitches often possess something which might be called personal taste in choice of partner, while almost all male dogs are prepared to mate with any bitch in season they meet. Any kind of lasting sexual engagement, a form of marriage, does not occur among dogs, but naturally a warlike male may keep other males at bay when a bitch is in season. In the wolf, on the other hand, one may well talk in terms of marriage. The male wolf brings prey to the lair, sometimes even to the cubs. The circumstances under which dogs live preclude the possibility of controlling whether any of this behaviour remains in dogs. But male dogs have no positive reaction to pups in 'home circumstances', apart from the fact that they are inhibited against acting aggressively towards them.

As in most mammals, and in birds, a dog's mating behaviour also involves the male carefully biting the female in the neck. In addition, if mating is allowed to take place quite undisturbed, the male usually gently licks the bitch, mostly round the eyes and ears. After the actual act of mating, the male and the bitch may still stay close together. It is possible that man's intervention just after the actual act has been completed—it takes up to half an hour—is one of the reasons why the two partners do not become involved with each other more deeply, for safe covering of a bitch requires only one completed mating, but several matings would perhaps lead to stronger ties between the bitch and her mate.

During the time when a bitch is sexually inactive she shows either no sexual behaviour whatsoever, or else in certain situations mild male behaviour in the form of weak or more pronounced mounting actions and an inclination to leg-lifting when urinating. A bitch in season may sometimes release in other bitches repeated mounting and neck-biting. In their turn, bitches in season may carry out the same actions with bitches not in season. A bitch not in season, however, does not invite mounting behaviour, but may allow a bitch in season to mount her. Some bitches are thus inclined to male actions when the female sex hormones do nor activate specifically female behaviour. Bitches' male behaviour, however, has such strong physiological motivation that it is hardly possible to stop it, and neither is there any ethological or physiological reason to intervene with such behaviour. In male dogs, the mounting of other dogs of the same sex is considerably rarer than in bitches. The reason for this may be the fact that male dogs are more aggressive towards each other, or that male sexual behaviour is activated all the year round through the production of male sex hormones.

A bitch's season usually occurs in the early spring and the autumn. If one owns two bitches, it is quite usual for their seasons to synchronise. My dachshunds at first came into season at quite different times, the mother every six months and the daughter every eight months. But when once the time coincided, they became synchronised, at which the daughter's began about a week after the mother's. It seems to me unlikely that in this case it is a matter of the mother's influence on the daughter, but perhaps happens through the agency of the olfactory sense and something which might be called mental influence. The hypophysis is obviously activated and its hormones then influence the sex hormones, but this has not been investigated, though the explanation is physiologically possible.

Sexual disturbances of the type that would complicate mating seem to be very rare in dogs. But it does happen that a bitch is so aggressive and dominant in relations to the required male that the male quite simply does not dare mount her. It also happens sometimes that the male does not bother about bitches of a certain breed of which he has had negative experiences, however friendly or inviting the particular bitch may be herself. In situations like this it is unlikely that covering will be successful. The male simply cannot ever 'ignore' the fear which the bitch releases and which inhibits sexual behaviour completely.

A calm and contented atmosphere combined with expectation may sensitise dogs to stimuli which lead to sexual behaviour. In face of a promised but not immediately imminent 'trip to the country', my older dachshund regularly reacts with de-lousing behaviour, with a blanket, for instance. This is anticipatory activity and this behaviour has no function in this situation. De-lousing behaviour is clearly almost identical in action to the neck-biting in mating. Through the de-lousing activity, the bitch is linked to a wholly different sphere of function: male sexual

G

behaviour with substitute objects, quite irrespective of which stage the bitch's sex-cycle happens to be at. A dog may thus also react to scents, the origin of which is not another dog, and its sexual behaviour can in this way be directed towards people.

PREGNANCY, WHELPING AND PUPS

Behaviour during pregnancy

Just before whelping some bitches show a very marked inclination to 'build a nest'. She scratches round with her forepaws in the bed, twists round, pushes the bedclothes about with her nose, and may even fetch 'nest-material' such as a blanket to the bed. Sometimes she carries out this activity out of doors as well. But a bitch does not seek to get away from people when whelping is imminent. A cat, which is far less domesticated, does retreat beyond the reach of people when its kittens are due. An inclination to hide food which a bitch would not otherwise hide may occur during the weeks before whelping. Strange dogs release more aggression than usual, especially if they approach her bed or food. In her bed a pregnant bitch may sometimes behave aggressively towards people whom she normally greets with the greatest joy. I have observed that my dachshund bitch also shows an increased inclination to react to objects that in some respects might resemble a pup, such as a soft toy of about the same size, as well as to whining noises. Individual variations in behaviour which deviates from the norm shown by a bitch during the days before whelping are very great, however, and many bitches do not behave noticeably differently from usual during this time.

False pregnancy

Bitches which have not conceived very often become falsely pregnant during the time when the pups should have been developing and when they should have been born. The milk glands

swell, and in some bitches even become well filled. The skin of
the belly is loose and dugs enlarged. Discharging from the vagina
occurs, and at the same time the bitch shows the same behaviour
that would occur in a real pregnancy. In this condition, a bitch
may easily accept strange new-born pups and presumably also
begin to suckle them. Whether she can then successfully foster
strange pups does not appear in ethological literature. Milk-gland
activity in false pregnancy usually ceases after two weeks from the
time when the pups should have been born.

Birth of pups and the bitch's reactions to them

When birth is iminent, a bitch is often uneasy. She lies down in the
bed, fidgets, wanders about, goes back to the bed, refuses food and
is not interested in walks. During her pains, a bitch has a very
characteristic facial expression, apparently fixing her stare on something nearby. Her tail, too, is held in a very typical way. Bitches
with straight tails hold them stretched straight out but bent sharply
down at the tip. Delivery may take an hour or so, but can go on for
twelve hours. The pause between each pup is usually long enough
for the bitch to have plenty of time to clean the first pup before the
next is born. Sometimes the pups are born so quickly that the bitch
has no time to carry out these cleansing actions. One should then
immediately uncover at least the nose and mouth of the pup the
bitch has not had time to deal with. It is not necessary to have any
veterinary training for this, but it is not part of this purely ethological book to offer veterinary advice. So get in touch with the vet at
the slightest worrying symptom before and during whelping!

It is by no means certain that a bitch will remain in the bed
when giving birth. This may have different origins, either the
remnants of behaviour, expedient in a wolf, which stops the bed
becoming soiled, or else a dog has lost the reaction of keeping to its
bed. It may even be that the sleeping place and whelping place
should not be the same, or that the whelping place does not satisfy
some demand unknown to us. During her pains the bitch ignores

the pups which have already been born. Similarly the pup just born and not yet cleaned blocks the bitch's reactions to the cleaned pups. It may happen, however, that disturbances in this behaviour's order occur, and then one must intervene, of course.

As soon as the pup, enclosed in its embryonic membrane, is born, the bitch pulls the 'pup-pocket' towards her, bites through the membrane, eats it and swiftly and energetically licks the pup clean. The navel cord is also bitten off. Then the pup has to find its own way to the mother's dugs. The route is short, for the bitch usually cleans the pup quite close to her own belly. It seems as if the bitch has no action which would push the pup towards her dugs, but she lies so that the pup succeeds in making its way to the mother's belly with those reflexes it has at its disposal.

A bitch will easily take her pups from one place to another, and when she does, she takes only one pup at a time in her mouth. On the other hand, I have never seen bitches carrying pups by the scruff of their necks, although this is a good way of lifting them. With the pup in her mouth, the bitch then wanders solemnly and with extreme care off to a place she has clearly chosen from memory. She does not look for a suitable place with the pup in her mouth, but takes it straight to a suitable place. Her tail is held low (in breeds with straight tails) and ears slightly back—a kind of creeping look. The pup is left alone and she goes back for the next one, and so on.

Most bitches have an extremely strong disposition to remain with their new-born pups, and some flatly refuse to be taken for a walk for the first few days after whelping. As soon as they have answered their need, they want to go back to the pups at any price. Bitches with this disposition are usually also very good mothers, have plenty of milk and accept pups even when they have grown bigger. It has been shown that a bitch's strong inclination to tend her pups is connected with the pups' characteristics and is not only dependent on the mother's physiological condition. If a bitch whose pups have already begun to eat food alongside their mother's milk is given new-born pups to care for instead of her own, for a couple of days she immediately reverts to the extremely regular tending behaviour which she normally only shows during the first few days after birth.

The characteristic carrot-like smell of pups seems to be an important releasing factor for adult dogs' reactions to them. A bitch cleaning a new-born pup has an expression which one might characterise as simultaneously one of the disgust and of the attraction the pup exercises over her. A bitch which has no pups of her own and is so friendly with a bitch with pups that she is tolerated in the pups' presence, shows great interest in the new-born pups, but usually cannot bring herself to lick them or tend them. My younger dachshund bitch (aged two at the time) walked with extreme caution, her neck outstretched, and her ears back, towards her mother's newly born pups, and began to dribble profusely. This was repeated occasionally for a few days, but after that she soon went over to full tending behaviour, but had no milk. At the time, the two bitches did not come into season simultaneously, otherwise both would have suckled the pups. One presumes that the strong scent of the pups constitutes protection against the interest of an approaching dog which itself is not in a physiological condition in which tending behaviour can be released. Male dogs also find pups, or their smell, interesting, but at the same time very unpleasant. No doubt the smell of a wolf's cubs constitutes a protection against the possible inclination of male wolves to eat their new-born offspring.

Reactions of new-born pups

A newly born pup, blind, deaf and smelling of carrots, is a completely helpless creature, its movements and reactions purely reflexes. When warm, a pup is quite quiet and immobile. Pups lie close together and keep each other sufficiently warm in this way, but if it is cold, a pup grows uneasy, creeps forward and whines. When something touches the pup's nose, it swings its head from side to side, in this way finding its mother's dugs. When suckling, the pup pushes itself forward with its hindlegs and presses on the milk gland with its forepaws. So a pup has all the essential reflexes typical of all mammals. From the very beginning, sucking is efficient and the tongue and gum together form a sucking funnel. During suckling, the pup holds its tail in the same somewhat lowered position as an adult dog does when eating.

Investigations into electrical activity in the cortex of the brain in pups show that higher brain functions are quite absent during the first ten days. The cortex is equally inactive when the pup is awake, as when it is asleep. Not until the pup is about twenty days old does any marked increase in brain activity appear when it is awake and moving. What a pup does during the first fifteen to twenty days is directed without the involvement of cortex centra. During the first ten days, the pup is a 'reflex animal' entirely, then follows a kind of transition period and at the same time the pup grows rapidly stronger. At birth, a pup's eyes are more or less closed, and they open gradually during the infant period's latter half. At about ten days, the pup begins to react to light, and within a few days to mildly contrasting visual impressions. The pupil reflex, however, is already in existence at birth. At first the cornea is semi-opaquely bluish, and becomes fully transparent within about five weeks.

During the infant and transition period pups normally urinate only when the mother licks their bellies. She does this very intensively and often rolls them over on to their backs so that no urine soils the bed. The mother's movements are swift and powerful and one has the impression that she does not carry out the actions until she senses the smell of urine. Excrement is also consumed very thoroughly. If the mother carries out normal tending actions, the pups' bed is kept very clean during the first two weeks, although the pups never leave it.

When the pup is twenty to twenty-two days old it begins to react to sounds. The first sign of this is when the pup starts at loud bangs or when the mother barks. At about the same time it also shows the first signs that it is going to be able to prick up its ears.

From the time when both sight and hearing have come into

function onwards, the pup develops swiftly both physically and mentally. Deviations from a wolf-cub's development are insignificant and different dog breeds show roughly the same speed of development, but at the same time there are individual variations. Many of the differences which characterise the temperament of different breeds also appear before the pup is four weeks old. Wolf-cubs suckle their mothers until the thirty-eighth or thirty-ninth day. Pups can if necessary manage without their mother or bottle-feeding from about four weeks. At this age they can drink, or rather lick up fluid food, and try to chew and swallow very small pieces of more solid food. The sharp milk-teeth of a pup make the mother reluctant to fulfil larger pups' clamouring demands for milk. It may happen, however, that some bitches allow pups to suckle at least occasionally up to seventy days. When the pups are scarcely four weeks old, they often jump up towards the mother, who begins to suckle them sitting, and later also standing.

In a wolf, the female stops cleaning and licking her cubs when they are four weeks old. Before that, the pups have grown sufficiently to move around on their own outside their bed. A two-week-old pup can walk wobblingly and slowly, a four-week-old already wanders about on its own in a room and looks for its mother if she is in the room, if only mostly in the form of erratic straying. At this age, the pups whine with slight indications of barking if they are cold, or if they have lost contact for a few minutes with the mother, or a person, or the other pups. During the whole of the pup's growing period, the mother reacts intensively if she hears the pups whine or cry out. To some extent a bitch can tell what has happened from the type of whine. She gets very worried at cries and becomes aggressive, but at whines she lies down with the pups. Other bitches which have no pups are also strongly attracted by the cries and whining of pups.

As soon as a pup actively starts moving about outside the bed, it also starts moving away from the bed to urinate. But the bitch usually cleans up after her pups even after they begin to move round a room. The reaction of licking the pup and getting it to urinate thus gradually disappears. During the fourth week, the first traces of what becomes play appear and at the same time the first attempts at aggressive barking are heard. These are, however, only very short, small, and apparently spontaneous outbreaks of these moods. It also happens that impressions which later have no play-releasing effects at all make a pup growl and bark or even rush

A very small pup reacts with swimming movements if it is held over water. Its legs straddle and move rhythmically and its tail swings jerkily from side to side.

forward, only to ignore completely at once whatever released this behaviour. The first clear tail-wagging may sometimes appear in pups that are only about two weeks old. At five weeks tail-wagging is usually quite common. As soon as the pup can walk, it can also swim, although its paws cannot give it sufficient speed for swimming to be of any practical use for the first five weeks. My younger dachshund bitch jumped into the water and swam out after us when she was only six weeks old. At four to five weeks the pup reacts with swimming motions if you hold it out over water, in a bath, for instance, even if it has never before been in contact with water.

A bitch's behaviour towards her growing pups entails only a few types of actions. Guarding behaviour is not so fixed as during the first days. Grooming behaviour decreases rapidly, suckling gradually becomes more and more spasmodic, and occurs mostly in places other than the bed. A bitch's ability to entice her pups to her is weak. The pups go to the mother because they are hungry or cold or are in a playful mood or because they are afraid, but not because the mother entices them to her. I have never heard any sounds which the pups would react to and which only have the function of enticing the pups to the mother. Instead, the pup begins to react to all the mother's sounds, her steps and the sight of her. When they are six to seven weeks old, pups are already able to move together with the mother, and follow her. At the same time the inclination to play increases greatly.

Imprinting

When a pup begins to react to other dogs or to people who appear in its field of vision, it has reached the beginning of a mentally very decisive period of its life. It is in fact through repeated confrontations with people that a pup acquires those characteristics which will make it trustful and friendly towards humans. It is said that a pup is imprinted by man. But a pup is also imprinted, if the opportunity arises, by its mother, by its siblings in the litter, and by other dogs in the environment in which it grows up. What does this imprinting entail, this process which American ethological literature calls socialisation? Schematically, one could say that imprinting entails an irreversible learning process through which a pup begins to direct the instinctive activity specific of its species and necessary to the social life of that species, towards the right objective, in other words towards its own species and towards objects, etc., in the environment which make this activity purposeful.

Instinctive activity of this kind is carried out without any learning process, identically by all individuals (taking age, sex, physiological condition, etc., into consideration). But part of the releasing mechanism of instinctive activity is not hereditarily sufficiently thoroughly adjusted to just those stimuli which make the behaviour purposeful, in fact directed at the 'right' objective. Imprinting entails a kind of learning process in which the central nervous releasing mechanism is complemented or limited, so that it is for ever irreversibly adjusted to the 'right' stimuli. In nature, mammal and bird young are imprinted almost without exception by their own species, its vocalisations, movements and markings, and by phenomena within the normal environment of that species. When a young mammal or a bird is reared, so that it loses its timidity and attaches itself to a person, this entails some part of the actions which would normally regulate the animal's behaviour towards its own species, instead being directed towards humans. Imprinting can either be concerned solely with actions typical of the growing period, or with the release of those actions which the adult animal in normal cases uses throughout its life in its relations to members of its own species. In most cases imprinting occurs at a very early stage. Larger adult wild mammals can seldom be made to accept a human being as a social companion. They may lose their timidity, but they do not become trustingly tame. They may even learn to seek protection or food from humans without reacting at all to humans in the way they react to members of their own species.

The reason why one should preferably take over pups while they are quite small is naturally that imprinting by a human being or a limited group of humans should come about. But a dog need not be imprinted solely by a person or people. On the contrary, a dog which has grown up among people and other dogs is often singularly trustful. The pup and its mother, and the human family, for instance, make up together in that case a kind of pack, and relations which are stabilised in this pack are very firm. It can also happen that the bitch's presence during the pup's development is devoted to making the pup's environment optimal with respect to imprinting. Naturally it is difficult for a human being to take the mother's place entirely in the life of a young dog, but it is considerably easier to take the place of the pack-leader.

A dog is receptive to imprinting from the end of the third week, but at this age the pup is naturally not yet developed enough that it can be taken from its mother. Only if the mother's milk dries up, should (and ought!) the pup be taken in hand and fed artificially from such an early age. Imprinting by humans occurs quite satisfactorily if the pup is taken in hand before it is two months old, and three months is in many cases quite acceptable. The sensitive period for imprinting is considered to cease at five to six months, but there are no exact investigations into this. It is also probably true that different breeds behave very differently. In comparison with other animals, the pup is receptive to imprinting over a strikingly long period, which naturally must be a result of selection principles in domestication. Wolf-cubs can be imprinted by humans if they are taken in hand at the time their eyes open.

Within reasonable limits, the more one has to do with the pup, the more powerfully it is imprinted by humans. Dogs which grow up in kennels usually have very little contact with people at all, with the result that kennel dogs and dogs generally which are not taken in hand by humans until they are over six months, are only slightly, if at all, imprinted by them. Under certain circumstances, this lack of imprinting may lead to extremely serious disturbances. An investigation has been made into about ten known cases in which dogs from different parts of Europe had attacked human beings, often their owners, and savaged them to death. Over half of these dogs, which had attacked their keepers or other people in their environment, were typical kennel dogs with no real contact with people during their youth. In the remaining cases, with one or two exceptions, they were psychically defective dogs, i.e. dogs which showed clearly abnormal reactions to their fellows as well. Dogs which are normal in their behaviour and which have grown up together with people, and thus are clearly imprinted by human beings, have only very rarely indeed been involved in this kind of deplorable event.

Dogs in packs, however, may possibly be thought to show a disposition to allow their aggression to transfer to the first best non-flight-releasing object, through an aggression which is really directed against a member of the pack. This may be the explanation for two cases in which dogs have killed children. Examples of aggression against a third and quite innocent party are common enough in the world of man. Among birds it is an everyday occurrence. Finally, it should be stressed that flight releases the hunting-action of chase. This may add to the statistics on the cases of dogs seriously or fatally savaging people. But considering the enormous number of dogs, how little people in general know about dog behaviour, and how very few accidents of this kind do happen, it must be said that domestic and sporting dogs fulfil extraordinarily large claims to harmlessness. Practically no object in a normal home is so harmless as a well-brought-up and correctly treated dog. There is, nevertheless, good reason to stress the need for domestic dogs, especially those which often come into contact with children, to be allowed to grow up in an environment in which good imprinting by human beings comes about.

The results of imprinting are in some respects different in different breeds. Some breeds seem to be very easily imprinted, others less so. Some become through imprinting extremely strongly tied to one single person in their environment (without, however, becoming dangerous for other members of the family), while other breeds with almost no imprinting by humans are always and everywhere just as friendly towards all friendly people they meet. Some of these dogs are also, unfortunately, friendly towards all people, without any exceptions, which is not especially desirable. Setters, pointers, spaniels and other game-dogs related to them, have a reputation for being friendly and rarely aggressive. Pomeranians of all kinds, Alsatians and Rottweilers are, on the other hand, pronouncedly one-man dogs. Imprinting in typical one-man dogs can happen so quickly that a single day or even one hour with a particular person makes the dog for ever inclined to regard just that particular person as its master. My first dachshund was imprinted by a person who handled it for three hours when it was six weeks old. This dachshund later on greeted this man in a much more friendly way than it greeted me, although his share in caring for this dachshund had been having it at home in a basket for three hours and feeding it once! The dog was not intended by the family to become in this way a 'two-home dog', but imprinting by members of the family, however, created no difficulties. The dachshund is not a pronouncedly one-man dog. This is also true of terriers. Terriers and dachshunds are pronouncedly family dogs when it comes to imprinting characteristics, and towards strangers they show aversion in varying degrees, sometimes pure aggression.

Imprinting has nothing to do with the true rearing of a dog. Consistency in rearing and a firmness which corresponds to a dog's disposition and future use do not in any way hinder imprinting. A growing pup is treated quite roughly by its mother and if it happens to land up with strange dogs it may well be even more brutally treated, even if it is not exposed to dangerous violence. Despite this, imprinting by other dogs, for instance in a kennel, is obviously thoroughly completed. One may presume that imprinting occurs most purposefully and easily if relations between the growing pup and its mother include a greater striving for contact than is normal between a mother and her pup. It is possible that the extension of the imprinting period to several months in dogs is a result of the fact that humans at all times have liked handling pups over a much longer period of time than that which a female wolf spends on her cubs.

Wolves which have been imprinted by humans may become dangerous to humans when they reach sexual maturity, if they are not treated so that they have not the slightest chance of seizing the pack-leader position from humans. In a wolf's life, it is quite normal that young animals sooner or later try to seize a high rank order in the pack. Tame wolves, especially males, may make attempts to become leader even if they have to oppose humans by whom they have been imprinted and against whom during this struggle for power (from a wolf viewpoint) they also show quite satisfactory social inhibitions. A wolf's struggle for higher rank is achieved with such rough measures that a person can be very severely savaged by the wolf's bite, while the same behaviour directed at another wolf would simply cause a few surface scratches. Neither can humans inhibit a wolf's aggressiveness through appeasement behaviour, which naturally a subordinate wolf would soon use in such a fight. If a human tries to resist a wolf, this increases the wolf's aggressive mood. Gustav Kramer, the German ethologist, found himself in a very dangerous situation when his tame wolf tried to take over the leadership in a struggle, with means considered quite valid in the wolf world. The wolf had to be shot to avoid Kramer being savaged to death.

Dogs have also very occasionally shown an inclination to try in this way to take over the leadership from humans. It is a matter of rearing to see to it that a dog is definitely kept in its place when it comes to social rank order. Most dogs create little difficulty in this respect, but there are some which demand a great deal of common sense and a certain harshness in treatment—naturally combined with friendliness and rewards. For some owners, it is hard to show this common sense, for others this vital turning-point creates no difficulties. I have the impression that it is primarily in association with play that the behaviour of young dogs, especially males, can show a tendency to pass into a struggle for power of quite an aggressive kind. When a dog shows an inclination to play roughly with its owner's footwear (on his foot!) or with his hands and does not willingly stop, this is an early stage in the struggle for power of the same type in which Kramer was involved with his tame wolf. Make sure that your dog does not get its own way! The kind of dog which in rank order will always be subordinate to its master, in the right hands is a happy dog, while on the other hand, a dog which mostly receives orders that it does not always obey presumably lives in an environment which is not especially suitable. It is a perfectly natural situation for a dog to have the pack-leader over it. Not even a small dog should be allowed to take over power in the family, even if its exercising of that power is insignificant.

During this imprinting period, a pup develops very quickly in all respects. Beyond what has already been mentioned, at six weeks pups begin to become interested in objects in their surroundings, sniffing at them and biting them. Then they begin to follow one another, walking in line. Tail-wagging soon becomes one of their most common actions. The inclination to lick the mother or humans in the face develops at the end of the suckling period. The hungrier a pup is, the more it shows this inclination to lick. Pups are usually fed by humans as soon as they no longer receive or no longer are allowed milk from the mother. So very few dog-owners have seen a bitch react by regurgitating food when a pup licks her mouth region. Under experimental conditions, in which the mother is in charge of the care of her pups after the suckling period, the bitch reacts in exactly the same way as a female wolf to her cubs' begging-licking.

Young dogs

During a young dog's life, a dog's interest in its surroundings increases very markedly. A pup reacts to sounds and objects without at first having any conception of either distance or direction. A young dog, however, has a very pronounced sense of space and it also rapidly learns that some noises, objects, etc., are uninteresting and others very significant. When the pup is fourteen to sixteen weeks old, its aggressive behaviour begins to liken that of an adult dog. Display and appeasement behaviour have matured and conflicts become mainly demonstrations of dominance or subordinance. The inclination to defend objects from other dogs becomes more and more pronounced and gradually territorial behaviour develops. The first clear expression of this is that a young dog not only defends objects, but also a small, gradually increasing territory round some object with which the dog likes occupying itself. Play and investigations into its surroundings are very conspicuous, and a dog's activity during this youthful period is greater than at any other stage of its life.

This period comes to an end when the dog becomes sexually mature. Bitches usually come into season for the first time at between six and nine months, and male dogs usually become sexually mature at about nine months, though there are considerable variations. As long as a male dog does not cock its own leg, then neither does it react much to other dogs' territory-markings and is largely ignored by these dogs. But this behaviour matures very suddenly. When the young male dog begins to cock its leg, it is, at least in normal cases, largely sexually mature and is no longer regarded by other dogs as a pup. At the end of this period, a wild animal would be gaining more and more experience of an increasingly large hunting territory, as well as experience of prey and hunting methods, gradually becoming a self-supporting individual in a pack. In a dog, which lives in conditions which make no demands in this direction, this youthful period has become much shorter. Female wolves become sexually mature when they are two years old, and males not until they are three.

In its relations to humans, on the other hand, a dog remains for the whole of its life at the stage which in many respects is much like a wolf's youth. Domestication very greatly extended the period during which a dog shows instinctive actions that are typical of a young dog, but has meant that sexual maturity and associated behaviour appear far earlier than in its wild ancestor. Many dogs' relations to humans seem to me to bear a considerable likeness to the relations between a young wolf and its mother. A certain lack of independence, an inclination to remain close to humans, an inclination to lick towards the face, great playfulness and an often pronounced submissiveness (many exceptions!) are features which without doubt can be described as appertaining to pups or young dogs. The fact that at the same time a dog—if it concerns individuals which are rougher, as long as humans allow it—tends to appear dominant towards other dogs and even towards humans, does not really contradict the above.

But possibly the combination of sharpness in temperament and the simultaneous presence of actions of young-dog type entails that it is not simple to decide from a dog's behaviour whether in some situations it may resist its master. Lack of imprinting does not necessarily show in a dog's everyday behaviour. A kennel-dog may be very friendly and very compliant, but still when it comes to social inhibitions may be unadaptable to humans. It must be pointed out, however, that no consistent reliable investigations have been made into the whole problem complex of the infantile features of a dog and imprinting of pups by humans. Well-known ethologists have in different contexts touched on the imprinting of dogs, but there has been no deeper research with more extensive material on this question. So what I have mentioned hitherto is only thoughts which have crystallised after considering existing ethological works and growing up in a home with dogs and then later always keeping dogs myself. Research has highlighted the great importance of imprinting, but many details on the rôle it plays for a dog and for dogs of different breeds are still lacking. This section on imprinting is intended to give readers an incentive to make their own observations and interpretations.

Play behaviour in pups and young dogs

Families with a dog watch the development of a pup with intense interest. At six weeks, a normal pup begins to growl and lift its foreleg towards its counterpart, though often with the result that it loses its balance. These actions, which in themselves are part of aggressive behaviour, are also the first actions which might be described as play. With this, a pup has also reached an age when we can and ought to devote to it care apart from purely physical care. In the life of a pup and a young dog, games play an important rôle, or at least ought to. Many dogs go on playing games, some even into old

H

age. It is important not to neglect playing with your dog, as its games also provide interesting opportunities for observation, and playing with people is to a very great extent concerned with binding a pup or a young dog to its master. This close contact probably encourages imprinting by humans, or at least imprinting by the person who looks after the pup.

Play behaviour has been described in several different ways. Amongst others, it is said that play is an activity during which the animal carries out actions, essentially innate actions, without the moods which normally follow or release these actions appearing. Playing-mood thus entails that with instinctive actions the animal manipulates what it commands without these actions being considered for the actions' real purpose and with no appetitive behaviour for the actions' real function existing. Thus one might say that playing is a kind of instinctive activity with no specific actions of its own.

Play-mood brings with it, however, pronounced appetitive behaviour for the actual game: the animal (or the human child) looks very actively for objects to play with in the most varying ways. A dog, like a human child (or an adult!) has its special favourite toys. The very sight of these toys may release play-mood, while conversely play-mood may cause the dog to look for its toys. Dogs very much like playing with objects that would not attract them if they had to carry out the same actions 'in earnest'. Favourite dog-toys are bits of wood, balls, pieces of rope, shoes, rags, etc. An important element in many games is the shaking of the toy, pure hunting behaviour. But if a dog begins to play with something like an old bleached bone, it may happen that the play-mood gradually passes into moods which the weak remnants of the scent of meat gradually release. Then the game suddenly becomes serious, and from having growled 'for fun', the dog suddenly growls in earnest at whoever its best playmate was a moment earlier. During real play, a dog retains its social inhibitions. A dog may, for instance, play with a person's hand without risk of its teeth gripping too hard. My dachshunds can play with my hand so that I can hook my forefingers behind their canine teeth. The game is wholly adapted to what my finger will tolerate. But if I play the same game with my finger inside a roll of paper, the dachshund no longer has any social inhibition against biting. It does not understand that the finger is inside the roll. If, however, the hand is protected by a glove instead, then the inhibition is complete.

Characteristic of a dog's behaviour when playing is that the dog can be very easily distracted, so that it stops playing. In a game entailing fighting behaviour or mounting actions, only some very insignificant impulse of another kind is necessary for the game to be replaced with behaviour associated with that new impulse. Real fighting mood and real sexual assault, on the other hand, are continuous and difficult to suppress as long as what releases them, another dog perhaps, is nearby.

A dog's games, however, contain not only innate instinctive actions, but to a greater or lesser extent also those actions which a dog has happened to carry out and which have led to the release of some inborn action. It may happen that a dog plays so that it jumps up on to something like a chair with a ball and then pushes

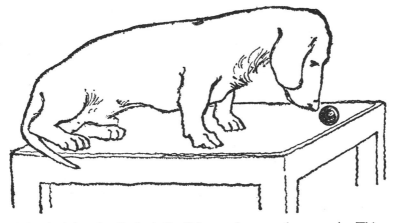

The dachshund rolls the ball off the stool over and over again. This is a game which the dog has learnt and which does not demand a playmate.

the ball off with its nose so that it rolls away, which at once releases the hunting instinctive action 'catch prey', but is carried out only in play. The dog runs after the ball, shakes it perhaps for a while, or throws it up in the air (an element in wolf behaviour when it has caught small prey), at which it returns to the chair, jumps up, pushes the ball over the edge, and jumps down after it. It can sometimes repeat this behaviour ten times in succession. The very fact that the dog does not know beforehand in which direction the ball will roll appears to stimulate the action. Mild excitement like this seems to be something positive in a dog's mind.

An even stranger game consists of the dog, without moving, giving a shove to a ball so that it rolls towards its man-partner, who then rolls the ball back to the dog. A ball-game like this, which can continue for several minutes, is hard to explain properly just from the understanding that the important part of play is that it contains instinctive actions. Has a dog in general some instinctive action, or even some taxes, which entail that with a shove of its nose it rolls an object in a desired direction? So play behaviour may in a dog, as in a number of other higher animals, contain elements which are unlikely to have anything to do with common instinctive actions. Dolphins and sea-lions obviously enjoy balancing objects on their noses, or carrying out other actions which have no particular function in their daily life. Crows find great satisfaction in making a loud noise with swaying (rope-ladder) fire-escapes, for instance. So animals with greater intellectual capacity can play in quite an advanced manner. A number of dog-games can also without doubt be described as intellectual achievements. Games of this kind entail a calm mood and so are very seldom played by dogs together. When a dog is alone, or together with a human being whom it trusts implicitly, but who in no way tries to excite the dog into some special mood, the dog may fall into a weak play-mood which may be expressed in games which contain acquired behaviour, and in which the games may also have a trace of intellectual achievement. On the other hand, the more the game entails pack-behaviour characteristics, the more it is dominated by innate actions of different kinds.

A dog's social games have been analysed quite thoroughly. In large terms, one can differentiate between games with contest-action dominance, games with hunting behaviour as dominating actions, and games which contain different kinds of social behaviour and other activity occurring in a group as their main elements. In these categories are the aforementioned much more variable ones, which in different dogs vary very greatly, and play behaviour which by no means occurs in all individuals, based on the use of acquired actions and the surprise element in the details of the actions involved in the game. Naturally the border-line between these different kinds of games is very indefinite. An analysis has been made recently of the Boxer's games, but this analysis lacks consideration of other types of games apart from social ones—and yet the Boxer presumably has the ability to play acquired games too.

In play behaviour, an action often suddenly peters out and another action intrudes instead. In order to analyse in detail the composition of the actions that make up games of contest, for instance, filming is necessary, for it is difficult to follow the shifting facial expressions and changes from one position to another with the naked eye. The importance of inquisitiveness, i.e. investigation, to the release of more common types of play has been emphasised. Dogs approach an unknown object and then carry out some action with the object which later in life they would carry out in activities such as hunting or fighting. An unknown but not too frightening object may release creeping and jumping, if the dog is in a strong play-mood, in the same way that a dog would hunt voles, or it may release gripping the object directly and shaking it in the same way that it shakes smaller mammals. Thus a dog follows in these games exactly the same 'instinct paths' that later find their definitive use in other circumstances. At only two months aggressive play activity is almost fully developed in a pup.

In some dogs, games with aggressive behaviour as the main

element dominate, in others prey-catching actions. Games in young dogs are thus composed primarily of actions which later dominate the dog's adult behaviour. The Boxer prefers to play so that it carries out actions associated with chasing and aggressive behaviour. As pups, my dachshunds, apart from aggressive games, showed an inclination very typical of their breed to dig in combination with their play. Terriers have a very pronounced inclination to play so that they pull with great violence in opposite directions any object which gives them a good grip with their teeth. Games of the latter kind occur with varying intensity in all dogs and are carried out so that the muscles are isotonally tense, so the dog does not fall over backwards if it suddenly loses its grip. With display behaviour, growling in time with tugs of varying strength, with less or more pronounced shaking and spurning with their paws, the pups try to wrench the object away from their opponent. If the game is in fact only play, success in these attempts leads only to the dog retaining the toy without even falling over backwards when it suddenly receives the toy without resistance. In this situation, however, the dog may begin to run away with the toy, in other words show play behavour of a non-aggressive kind. This running away with the toy probably contains many different kinds of behaviour, such as the mood to hide or carry away food, and in the chasers, partly general inclination to run with the toy (a kind of imitation), and partly an attempt to seize the toy.

In my older dachshund bitch, who is exceptionally uninterested in hunting, I have observed repeatedly one special type of play-mood but never in any of the other seven dogs I have known very well. We usually call this mood 'dachshund discovering nature', as the mood occurs only out of doors. The dog is calm and contented, but suddenly her interest is caught by some small thing nearby, an ant, for instance, or a red mite, a midge or a piece of bark on the surface of a pool, or by a mild chuckling sound of water on a stony shore. With great caution, her contented expression retained, and quite without fear, she goes very slowly, but not creeping, towards the place where the interesting object is, looks carefully at everything and especially the object, perhaps dipping her nose in the water and breathing out so that the water bubbles. During all this quiet investigation, she seems quite contented, slightly curious and very benign. The slightest comment or minutest event in the proximity, such as the cry of a tern, distracts her and the mood peters out. I would like to regard this as a kind of intellectual play-mood. The dog is investigating things which it knows quite definitively have no importance. The mood presupposes peace and quiet in sunny weather in an environment that the dog very much appreciates.

Dogs with great interest in hunting may perhaps in general be considered to have greater inclination to play even when older, while dogs with little interest in hunting do not show any pronounced hunting behaviour in the form of play either. Aggressively disposed dogs may well fall into a more and more aggressive mood while at play, at which the game gradually becomes rough. At the slightest sign of success in the opponent (if the opponent succeeds in seizing the toy, for instance) the mood passes from play into fighting. If the hairs along the back rise and the tail's position shows display behaviour, the dog is then fully prepared to defend or retrieve the toy aggressively, or else to subjugate its opponent by force. As soon as one of two dogs of differing strengths show this behaviour, however, the other's desire to play is subdued and the game ceases without conflict. It is rare for two playing dogs to fall into a mood simultaneously so that play passes into aggressive behaviour.

My dachshunds cannot play together for more than a few seconds with something like a rope which they pull in opposite directions. The game begins with typical play invitations, usually carried out by the older and stronger (the mother), but the daughter's play-mood is inclined to become aggressive during the game. This the daughter has learnt, and as soon as the mother growls, regardless of whether the growling is only part of pure play-mood, or the first sign of aggressive mood, the daughter's play-mood vanishes and she wanders off, often clearly disappointed. On the other hand, in play which does not contain actions from the sphere of aggressive behaviour, when one or both lie on their backs in appeasement postures, they may play for a long time together. So temperament and experience to a very great extent decide how far two older dogs can play with each other.

An invitation to play can hardly be misunderstood. It may be creeping carried out in a characteristically exaggerated manner, or the dog lowering its head on to its chest with its forelegs stretched out, or also the dog rolling over on its back, inviting play in this manner. A few swift jumps towards the other dog, the tail wagging and hind regions wriggling, is another typical play invitation. The ears are either laid back or raised and held close together across the head. The latter means that the inviter is in an extremely benign mood, but that the mood may contain sexual behaviour, and also most often that the inviter is dominant in relation to the dog to which the behaviour is directed. Dogs very quickly learn to bring toys to each other or to humans, and in this way invite them to play. Play invitation is the behaviour in which a dog's invitation actions are demonstrated most clearly. Barking and other vocalisations also belong to play invitation with very great individual variations.

Actions included in the sphere of play behaviour in adult dogs appear to pass very easily into actions included in sexual behaviour. Sexual mood in its turn, probably as anticipatory actions, gives rise to play behaviour. A play-mood may also, via very insignificant stimuli (or none at all?), pass into sexual mood or into de-lousing behaviour in soft objects, and in this way into sexual behaviour. Play and complicated forms of play invitation occur very generally as anticipatory behaviour in an expectant mood. Finally one can also say that all these actions are outbreaks of a certain mood of joyfulness.

Play of different kinds makes the growing pup or young dog more and more trustful towards its environment, including the dogs that are in this environment. Naturally these games also mean that the dog exercises its muscles. So one can presume that play behaviour of different kinds makes the individual better equipped, although it is hardly possible to prove this. Only in a few cases can acquired behaviour, which a dog more or less involuntarily incorporates in its play repertoire, be of any importance to the dog later on. Presumably this also appertains to the use wild animals make of their play behaviour.

3 ETHOLOGICAL CHARACTERISTICS AND LIMITATIONS

ASSOCIATION AND INTELLIGENCE

Many dog-owners ask themselves whether a dog has the ability to manipulate memories in such a way that without previous experience it can behave purposefully in situations in which its innate reactions are no use. The better one knows a dog and the more thoroughly one analyses dog behaviour, the more evident it becomes that in this respect the dog is not intelligent. Instead, a dog has an individually variable but usually considerable ability to behave purposefully with the starting-point of previous experience. A dog associates positive events and experiences of different kinds with what it has done before, or in connection with some unpleasant event. Thus a dog has a great capacity to associate details in its own behaviour with successes or failures of different kinds. But quite indifferent experiences also stay in its memory and can be used at some later stage.

An easily understood example of how associations develop can be shown in a dog's experiences in hunting. Under the influence of hunger and innate appetitive behaviour for instinctive actions used in hunting, a dog makes his way out into the terrain. At some place, it finds voles, for instance, which it catches and perhaps eats, or a hare which it begins to chase. The dog will then associate a number of different events and actions which it has experienced or carried out before it finally caught the voles or began to chase the hare in that successful hunt. The first time, it perhaps only begins to build a memory and association source which embraces only what the dog did just before it caught or found its prey. But the next time the dog is present at the same successful hunt, the chain of association may be widened to embrace events which perhaps occurred several hours before the conclusion. The next time the associations may widen, from a time point of view, even further back. So a hunting dog becomes extremely happy when it sees its master preparing for a hunting trip. And so preparations for these preparations, i.e. human beings discussing whether there is to be a hunting trip, are also associated with the anticipated trip. Every 'dog-owner builds up association chains such as these. The dog learns after only a few experiences what usually happens before some definite event. If this event is a positive experience, the dog does what it can to put itself in a position in which the event occurs. It tries to attract attention and carry out anticipatory actions as soon as its master does something which reminds the dog of preparations for what the dog associates the preparations with. If it is a negative experience, then the dog avoids everything that it associates with this unpleasant experience, and then also easily evades the conclusion itself, the unpleasant situation.

All dogs that are usually called 'clever' are in fact primarily experienced. A young dog is an inexperienced dog, and consequently is never 'clever' in that meaning of the word. It quite simply has not had time to acquire experience, and has not been able to build up chains of association which are the prerequisites for the dog behaving in a way that we in everyday speech, when it comes to dogs, call 'clever'. It is quite a different matter that a number of individual dogs have an especially great inclination to observe their surroundings and the behaviour of human beings, etc. Dogs with this disposition have a good starting-point for building long complicated chains of associations in which humans and their environment and behaviour may play a very large part. Dogs with not too lively a temperament clearly find it easier to build association chains firmly rooted in events in which humans play a part. Dogs which constantly live among humans and which hear humans speak (people often talk to their dogs, and so they should, as this is an important prerequisite for the dog becoming 'clever') gradually learn to associate words or short sentences with definite actions, objects and events. It is very common for a dog to react purposefully to about ten different words. With a little training, a dog can probably be made to 'understand' the meaning of a much larger number (up to about a hundred, according to Scott), or equally well a number of quite acceptable combinations of sounds which one uses in situations which are significant to the dog. With no consistent training, a dog learns most easily to react to words used in association with feeding, watering, walks, hunting trips, etc., and also to words which are used in situations in which a dog becomes aggressive or frightened. These words may have a specific meaning to the dog, such as describing a certain kind of food, or a certain kind of titbit, and if the dog does not receive just what it is 'promised' with the particular word, it may happen that it will be very disappointed.

But words can naturally also have a much wider meaning, for instance describing the place where titbits of varying kinds are kept, and then the dog is quite satisfied if it receives a titbit in the habitual place, irrespective of what the titbit is like. It is only the use and the association which decide what the dog expects when it hears a certain word. Naturally, we cannot imagine an exact representation of what a dog eventually receives in the way of a memory-picture when it hears a word like 'sausage', but that it does not, for instance in a 'sausage-eating mood', which is released in the dog by a marked pronunciation of the word 'sausage', want to eat an otherwise favoured toffee or perhaps even cheese, means, however, that the dog in fact receives from the word 'sausage' very concrete associations with just that kind of food that we call sausage. A dog's joyful vocalisations have different expressions in different moods, and there is reason to doubt that a dog in fact receives a concrete representation of positive events with which a word known to the dog creates association.

A domestic dog also gradually learns without any special training the names of different members of the family, and even those names of regular and welcome visitors. This association is probably most easily developed by the dog repeatedly hearing the person's name just before the person in question comes home or on a visit, and later when the person greets the dog with pleasure; in other words they are pleasure-denoting. Welcome visitors are in general also welcomed by the dog of the house, especially if the visitors themselves are also dog-owners. My dachshunds go to a member of the family when ordered to only if they can expect a reward, without which they do nothing. Friendliness is the least reward, and the best is that the family is to gather together round the dining-table.

The very varying joy reactions dogs show when they hear words of a certain content is evidence of how special a dog's associations can be. I have also made observations which I cannot interpret in any other way than that dogs can also enjoy the associations they receive in cases when the situation does not develop into a concrete experience, and when the dog does not expect that that will happen either. My older dachshund bitch can sometimes very pronouncedly exhort me to tell her something which she thinks is pleasant. Most especially, she likes to hear things which she associates with experiences and situations on our summer island. But a short 'story about the Christmas tree' also gives her great pleasure. The Christmas tree and its decorations give her positive associations, as she usually steals chocolates and toffees from the bottom branches of the Christmas tree, or at least attempts to. She also sometimes guards the tree, so that others shall not get at these objects. It is interesting that when she hears me talk about these interesting and very desirable things, she does not at all expect to travel to the country, or that the Christmas tree should at once appear in its traditional place in the house. She seems more to enjoy hearing me mention words which for her have positive

associations. This is much the same phenomenon as when a small
child enjoys hearing a familiar fairy story told over and over again.
When you stop telling the story, the dachshund asks you to go on,
nudging you with her nose, staring into your face and waiting for
you to repeat those many interesting words. But she doesn't go
over to the door or to the place where the Christmas tree usually
stands. Perhaps one can presume that she herself cannot receive
these Christmas-tree and summer-island associations whenever
she likes, but that she enjoys receiving them through a person
speaking of them.

It seems probable that to some extent a dog can manipulate
memories in a way that makes it possible for it in a certain mood to
choose between different memories and then behave in accordance
with some very special experience. A dog which suddenly, and for
reasons which are not easy to explain, falls into a play-mood, is
usually not content with the nearest toy, or with the nearest object
suitable for play, that is handy. On the contrary, a dog in a strong
play-mood usually seeks out extremely purposefully some very
special toy which perhaps it happened to see in some place several
days previously, perhaps out of doors. I feel it must be true that a
dog in a situation such as this in fact remembers very exactly both
that particular toy and where it last saw the toy in question. In the
same way, a dog will remember exactly where it has buried a bone,
where prey is, the routes it usually takes to places it usually visits,
and so on. Some additional association of a positive or negative
kind is obviously decisive for which alternative a dog chooses.

How long does a dog remember an event, an object or an
experience? The answer is often for the rest of its life, if when the
experience happened the dog had reached the young-dog stage and
especially if the experience was strongly effective. The very fact
that a wolf or a dog, which had been present at some place on a
successful hunt, later repeatedly visits exactly the same places, even
if there is no prey there any longer, shows how slowly a strong
association is forgotten. Checking over hunting-grounds, which at
some time or other have shown themselves to be advantageous, is

naturally also purposeful. It is possible that where there has once been prey, sooner or later there will once again be prey. The first thing my dachshund does on every visit to our summer island is to check the vole places, quite irrespective of whether it is a vole-year or whether that year there are no voles whatsoever.

A dog which has once learnt to know a person, recognises that person for the rest of its life. A dog which has once been badly treated by a person, finds it difficult to forget such a negative experience. Dogs which show an inclination to be unreliable towards certain categories of people (soldiers, children, drunks, or old ladies, to take a highly heterogeneous sample of people to whom some of my dogs have shown antipathy) have had some negative experience in which some individual of that human category has been deeply involved. So long as another person of the category in question, through a positive action, does not change the dog's attitude, which is based entirely on one single experience, the dog's aversion remains, though over the years its intensity lessens.

An important element in behaviour based on association chains in which humans play a part is that the dog makes its wishes comprehensible to the person. An action which concludes with the dog trying to clarify its wishes to a person is naturally not successful until the person fulfils the dog's wishes. This leads us into a dog's self-training. A dog's ability to train itself is equally as important as its ability to associate different events with each other and perhaps partly build on this. As an example of self-training, I will take a dog's well-known but not always approved of ability to beg for food, a simple example, and the ability to ask for its drinking-bowl to be refilled, a series of behavioural actions which are often mistakenly interpreted as intelligence.

A dog has an innate action of whining or barking when it cannot carry out an action which has strong motivation. It whines when it is hungry. Whining attracts attention and it is given food. Louder whining attracts attention more quickly than soft whining. A few situations in which a soft whine does not give results, but an increased intensity immediately makes a human fulfil the dog's wish, lead to a dog also reacting by whining or barking to mild hunger or cultivated 'miserliness' (food so attractive that even when a dog is satisfied the food releases the eating wish). Generally speaking, by regarding whining as a hunger signal, and by reacting more quickly to more intensive whining or barking than to insignificant whining, we give the dog every opportunity for self-training: 'The more noise I make the quicker I get the titbit.' If your dog begs loudly for food even if it is not exceptionally hungry, the reason is simply that you have been too weak, or perhaps you have not been completely consistent in the bringing up of your dog. Your reaction to the whining of a dog is natural, but once you let yourself be influenced by it, the dog naturally replies with an increase in the intensity of the behaviour which leads to success. Small punishments for begging now and again lead to no result except that the dog sometimes becomes slightly 'offended'. Neither does a dog give up a good hunting method, although it does not succeed in finding prey every time with just that method.

A dog which finds its drinking-bowl almost empty, licks the bowl quite dry, at which the bowl probably rattles against the floor. Whoever hears this noise naturally comes and fills the bowl, at which the dog drinks until its thirst is slaked. The next time the bowl is empty, first an association arises between the rattling noise which the bowl makes when empty and the fact that the dog then can slake its thirst. Then as soon as it finds the bowl is empty, the dog begins actively to push the bowl around so that it makes a noise, at which a human naturally reacts more quickly. The dog combines humans with drinking, then the different actions which a human carries out with the fact that the bowl is refilled and the dog can slake its thirst. Thus the association and self-training go step by step onwards until perhaps, when it finds the bowl empty, the dog quite simply picks up the bowl and takes it to the person who usually fills it. It would never happen that without this step-by-step self-training the dog would bring the bowl and ask to have it filled. On the other hand this is what a primate would probably do at once (if it did not fill the bowl itself from a tap), and perhaps also some other monkeys. But a dog cannot solve the problem through insight, and has to turn to lengthy self-training to reach the same goal.

A dog cannot just use its invitation behaviour to attract attention with the intention of making a person carry out an action which the dog itself will not take part in, but which will be only indirectly (or not at all) useful to the dog. A dog invites you to play, for instance, by running up to you with a toy and laying it down in front of you, by carrying out play actions with the toy, by barking or jumping

Begging takes many forms. In the author's dachshund the innate action 'scratching with the paw' had through self-training gradually developed into 'hanging over the foot'.

round you. It may nudge you with its nose or scratch you with its paw. Play invitations are usually composed of lively actions of different kinds. An invitation to 'come with me' (on a walk, for example) may contain actions such as the dog laying its nose in your lap, or by hanging its head, with the whole weight of the front of its body over your foot as you sit. Individual variations are very great. The dog invites you through different actions, but without any self-training, to take part in actions which dogs can normally carry out together. But it is only through self-training that a dog can learn to invite us to activity of the type that its

I

species does not normally indulge in. In all invitation behaviour there are both innate elements and elements which appear by chance (often through self-training). So invitation behaviour varies greatly in different dogs, even if a number of components are common to all.

Neither can a dog imitate our actions, for instance, in some experimental arrangements which would enable the dog itself, directly and with no previous self-training, to acquire a titbit by carrying out some simple action. A primate, on the other hand, in a similar experimental situation, would either soon imitate our behaviour (pressing a button, or opening a trapdoor, etc.) or see the possible solutions that the experimental arrangement offered. So a dog has no imitation ability, and the thought capacity which it may have is not sufficient for it to solve problems of this type. Association behaviour and mood transference between dogs lie on another level. When a dog learns to open a door, this is not imitation, but possibly an action which to some extent is connected with associative learning. The door shuts off a passage which others use. Faced with an obstacle, a dog is inclined to jump up, push away, etc., and if its paws happen to press down the door-handle, the actions that led to the passage becoming free are associated with this success. So the dog learns, through self-training, to open doors.

A dog's reaction to its own name is also a result of training or self-training. A dog associates the sound-combination which we use as a name for the dog with an alert situation which has positive content. We teach the dog to respond to its name and reward it clearly with pats, friendliness, etc., when it responds and comes to us. The reason why most dogs like being patted, at least by their owners, is not easy to find out, but one possibility is that some caresses and pats are accepted positively in the same way as some of a dog's own tending actions. I think the most important factor is, however, that at a very early age a dog associates people's caressing-behaviour with advantages to the dog itself—titbits, for instance, or anyhow a mood in which humans do not treat a dog harshly. On

top of this is that humans' friendly vocalisations become signs to a
dog that no danger threatens, so the dog can be calm, which may be
in itself is already a positive mood.

Most more advanced behaviour shown by a dog has been learnt
through different kinds of training, often through self-training of
the trial-and-error type. In comparison with success, failure is a
kind of punishment which leads to, the next time the situation is
repeated, a dog usually choosing to carry out the action which led
to success. This strengthens even more the inclination to
choose this alternative the next time, etc., etc. So when one
wishes to teach a dog something, it is a matter of placing it in a
position in which the desired action is rewarded. The undesired
alternative action or non-successful action should, on the other
hand, not entail active punishment. This would only lead to the dog
acquiring an attitude of strong aversion to the whole situation in
which one is trying to complete the training. When a wild wolf is
exposed to self-training, this occurs primarily so that the alternative
is not great success as against strong aversion-releasing or flight-
releasing situations, but so that the alternatives are uneventfulness
or indifferent experiences in a normal environment as against one
extreme or another, pronounced to a lesser or greater degree. Thus
all true punishment is wrong when one is to teach a dog something
new. But if it is a question of creating an association between
something the dog does, but should not be allowed to do, and a
mood of aversion, then a mild punishment is the natural method.
The difficulty is primarily in that the punishment or the unpleasantness should be right chronologically. The dog may easily
associate in an undesirable way, for instance, the punishment
with the place where the punishment took place, instead of the
punishment with the thing the dog happened to do in that place.
How easily a dog associates unpleasantness, in a faulty way from a
human point of view a purposeless way and from a training point
of view, appears when dogs which have nearly been run over
do not become afraid of cars in general, but afraid of the place
where the accident happened. Naturally a reward for a successful

reward for a successful effort should occur immediately, especially when this concerns young dogs.

One often hears of dogs having a bad conscience when they have done something they should not have done. This observation is doubtless quite correct, but the name of this mood is only correct if one uses the concept of bad conscience in the purely ethological-biological sense—fear of punishment. Bad conscience in humans pre-supposes moral values, even if the background is in the long run fear of unpleasantness of one kind or another. A dog cannot make such decisions and its bad conscience is pure fear. Thus a dog has a bad conscience when it has done something which it associates with punishment (unpleasantness) or (in more advanced cases) if what it has done results in unpleasantness if humans see the action in question. Dogs which have a great capacity for building up purposeful associations do not associate the action as such with the punishment but with the fact that the punishment is the conse-quence only if a person sees the dog actually do the actual deed. The association chain can be built on further: the dog is quite untroubled until it sees that a person is noticing or has noticed that the dog has done something it should not be allowed to do.

One of the leading figures in modern ethology, Konrad Lorenz, the founder of research into instinct, has in a few cases, however, found that bad conscience in dogs may lead to behaviour in which a certain ability to reflect must be presupposed. Perhaps a dog which does not appear to have the slightest thing on its conscience, although it has done something forbidden, genuinely actively tries to avoid punishment by doing things that are allowed but which also con-tain some elements in common with the forbidden behaviour! One of Lorenz's dogs sometimes used to attack a flock of hens which ate the remains of the dogs' food, which naturally annoyed the dog. But when it suddenly saw that its master was watching its activities, it continued on through the flock of hens without attempting to nip any of them, and instead barked at an imaginary enemy far away. The same dog sometimes barked by mistake at its master, but when it saw who he was, it ran to a wall behind which was another dog, and barked there instead. Although I have seen my own dogs do the same thing several times, I am not altogether certain that Lorenz's suggested explanation is the right one. Lorenz himself also points out that there could be other explanations, but he sticks to the one that presumes intelligent deliberation. Another possibility would be that it is a question of anticipatory behaviour, or possibly a question of sensitising for aggression-releasing stimuli. The barking could be thought to be the cause of the dog remembering some other thing that it usually barks at.

In dog literature, however, other forms of behaviour are also described, in which a dog's achievements seem to depend at least on manipulation with different alternatives to the solution of some problem. Lorenz describes how one of his bitches pretended to be lame to avoid bicycle trips. After an accident, the bitch had learnt that it did not have to run beside the fast bicycle so long as it limped, as then Lorenz got off and walked. The dog then used its limp as an excuse for walking even if its paw was not in the slightest sore. The following experiment is also worth mentioning. Without any previous experience, a dog was able to make its way through a labyrinthine arrangement with a system of doors which entailed that a middle door would have to be actively put in another position if the dog was to have room to turn so that it could reach the next door. So the dog saw what it would have to do to be successful, but it had previous experience of how doors functioned. A dog's ability to choose a shorter route in unknown territory only on the basis of an orientating look at a hindering fence can be interpreted as intellectual deliberation. But there is a great deal of evidence to show that dogs in general cannot understand simple 'connections'. Without being taught, no dog can pull towards it a piece of meat that is inaccessible but has a piece of string tied to it that the dog can reach. Neither can a dog ever carry out an action of the 'build-up-an-arrangement-to-reach-an-inaccessible-desired-object' type. No dog drags up a chair to a table to be able to steal food in this way—although the dog could easily pull or carry a suitable chair through a whole flat. Neither do dogs ever pull up a chair to a window, for instance, to be able to jump up on to the window-sill and look out. Actions of this type are regularly carried out by primates and by a number of other monkeys, at least occasionally. A dog's brain has obviously no particular capacity for manipulating thought-out changes in the environment. But dogs can use an action from a sphere of function in a (to some extent) new connection. My male Scottish terrier sometimes fetched a blanket from its bed to have a soft underlayer when lying in the sun on the floor. So the Scottie could use its nest-building behaviour extremely purposefully.

On the other hand one can perhaps presuppose a certain capacity for manipulating alternative memories. The case with the involved movement in the labyrinth of doors can perhaps be explained by the dog in question having so much experience of doors that it manipulated that experience, and realised that doors can be placed in different positions. But there is no explanation which quite covers the dog's behaviour without some intelligence being involved.

All my experience of dogs shows that when they carry out actions which might be considered intellectual efforts of the deliberation-on-alternatives type, one has reason to turn to the explanation based on the lowest intellectual achievement in dogs. To summarise, one might perhaps say that a dog has a very good memory, an excellent ability to observe, but no ability to imitate, an excellent ability to associate and a pronounced ability to produce and use memories of different kinds, under the influence of different moods, including memories of what it has experienced far back in time. Obviously a dog can also to some extent manipulate memories such as these and use them in new situations. On the other hand, a dog is not capable of refurbishing its memories or using them directly as a starting-point for non-innate behaviour. Neither can it think out the possible consequences some action, anatomically possible to a dog, might have. A memory which is the result of success in some action may, however, be used as the starting-point for some quite different behaviour. One and the same object, one and the same environment can thus have different functions for a dog according to the dog's mood. A dog clearly often remembers the environment and the object as free-standing memories of different kinds and these memories can be activated in many different ways through very different kinds of associations.

Dogs dream often and lengthily. It seems safe to say that when it barks, growls, whines or gives indications that it is running or wagging its tail, or carries out other movements and moves its eyes and ears in its sleep, a dog is in fact dreaming in the same way as a person dreams. My dachshunds' dream behaviour indicates very strongly that after especially interesting country experiences they dream much more vividly than when they have been living a quiet life in our city flat. So a dog's dreams would not be simply vacant activity of the brain, released when certain behaviour has not occurred for a long time. Instead, it seems to be a matter of activation of recently acquired strong memories of different kinds, a kind of free-thought-activity. Dogs react only with a certain surprise to each other's dream noises.

ORIENTATION

A dog which usually moves about in a limited area generally has little difficulty in finding its way home from anywhere within that area. Occasionally one hears it stated that dogs have sufficient capacity for orientation that if they are taken to a completely strange place, they can find their way home quite quickly. I have tried to decide to what extent these stories of dogs' long-distance orientation to home really contain anything which might be described as scientifically tenable criteria for an extreme ability to orientate. One is then immediately forced to make a weighty objection: there is a very large number of cases of dogs disappearing in unknown territory during their attempts to find their way home from unknown territory, but only a few cases in which dogs really have found their way home. In my view, this can interpreted in two ways: one, that it is pure chance if a dog finds its way home, and two, that the dog may in some way or other have learnt that its home usually lies in a certain direction, from its hunting-grounds, for instance.

If such a dog finds itself in an area unknown to it, it makes its way in the direction in question and may be lucky enough to have hit on the right way home. In each case the proximity of the home territory finally impinges through olfactory experiences, at which the dog presumably passes to an orientation form based on search reactions, until it reaches a place which it recognises in detail. One can start from the fact that a dog which is used to moving freely about in woods or forest can generally without difficulty find its way home from all places which it has visited from home on its own in a calm mood. In all probability it is firstly the countryside's scents, and secondly paths and roads that are in fact decisive.

It is known that a wolf's summer and domestic territory, in which the male habitually hunts and chooses an easy way home with its prey, may embrace some hundreds of square kilometres. During the time of year when wolves are on the move, in a number of regions they have a clear direction tendency in their movements. Wolves in Finland which occasionally wander in over the border also have these tendencies. It is perhaps not too bold to presume that these movements, not very specific but quite clearly orientated, are based on the use of the main directions of the moon or the sun. An ability of this kind to keep to a definite direction in unknown territory can be presumed to be inherent in at least some dogs, even if breed differences can be expected to be great. No one would expect a Pekingese, or any other small domestic dog, to have the same ability to orientate as a breed used regularly in hunting or shepherding in scattered areas. Selection in the origins of the breed and then within breeds has probably strongly influenced the ability to orientate in a dog. But a Pekingese is also able to stray several kilometres from its home and find its way back without difficulty. All breeds of dogs have obviously retained considerable ability to orientate efficiently within smaller areas round the home.

Orientation within larger areas is probably made easier by shores, lakes, streams and seas, by towns and industries, etc. Theoretically, it is not impossible that scents such as these, in combination with the direction of the moon and sun, give a dog plenty of opportunities for orientation, anyhow considerably more than we humans have without technical aids. Neither can the possibility be excluded that a dog, at about ten kilometres' distance, is also able to recognise some scent which indicates a direction when seeking its home.

After a few walks, every town dog knows the shortest way home in that labyrinth of city streets and tall buildings. In this way a dog builds up a kind of memory map over the territory it moves in. This memory map is naturally based on information received through all the dog's senses, but mostly its senses of smell and vision. Within the area which in this way a dog knows in detail, it can use short cuts to reach a certain point quickly (the home of a bitch in season, for example), or to get home as quickly as possible in bad weather. If the weather is fine, a dog may well choose to take especially long routes instead. This use of short cuts, however, is not evidence of advanced mental capacity. This capacity has been also found in experiments with rats and mice in labyrinths. But there is a difference between orientation in small spaces in which the memory of muscular effort, turnings, etc., may direct the animal, and orientation out in wild country. A dog by no means needs to go home at once—it may interrupt its wanderings, making minor diversions, and then go home by quite a different route from the one it had first 'thought' of taking.

Dogs which find themselves in strange territory generally look for roads and paths. If a wolf finds itself in strange territory, it naturally avoids paths and roads, perhaps primarily because they give off scents which the wolf associates with man-the-enemy. A dog's preference for paths and roads when it is not showing hunting behaviour may perhaps be due to the fact that man generally walks his dog somewhere associated with a network of roads. As far as I know, there have been no experiments to show whether a dog's preference for walking along roads is innate. One circumstance which also plays a part is that a disorientated dog usually looks for its master, and as people usually walk on roads, a dog looks for its master primarily on roads of different kinds. Preference for main roads may conduct dogs along long stretches and add to the fact that some dogs quickly find their way home, while others go in quite wrong directions instead.

There are several examples of a dog boarding a train or a boat by itself to get to some favoured place it has often visited together with its master. This behaviour is naturally based entirely on the fact that the journey has pleasant consequences: a visit to a desirable hunting-ground, perhaps. As long as the journey of the vehicle is not of long duration, a dog could thus easily make its way to the family's summer cottage, for instance. But in the confusion of modern traffic conditions, such excursions are doomed to failure. My dachshunds would in fact choose the right place for getting on a bus, but would not be able to choose either the correct bus-service or the right end-stop. A dog has very little capacity for choosing the right floor in a multi-storey building, if its home is several floors up. Not even the strange scents by doorways to the wrong flats make a dog go immediately to the next one. But a dog would under no circumstances choose a door which is not situated in the same position as the door of its own flat. So one gets the impression that the situation of the door in relation to the stairs is automatically noted, but the important question of how many floors up home is is not included in the things a dog simply learns. An important reason for this is probably that a dog does not usually go upstairs to a town flat alone, but with a member of the family. So there is no training for wrong-or-right flat.

Another important and probably more significant circumstance is that a dog lives in a world which normally cannot offer problems of the type involving counting the number of repetitions of identical but not simultaneously visible structures. Even out of doors, if several similar houses are close to each other, it may happen that a dog misses the right house and just goes on walking towards a correctly situated door in the wrong house. But if the dog is let free and is allowed to orientate on its own, it certainly won't miss the right door. A dog following its master can to some extent in this way switch off its ability to orientate in an area well known to the dog, but still reacts to a wall with doors situated exactly like those in its own home, or a stairway, as if it were outside its own home.

Summarising a dog's orientation, it can be said that a dog very quickly learns to know areas it regularly inhabits, and that within this area, it learns to use roundabout routes, short cuts, and easy connecting routes such as paths and roads. It walks, if it is allowed to and if it is not pronouncedly a guard dog, purposefully from its home to any point in the territory, if at that place there is something in which it is specially interested. It extends its territory almost unlimitedly when necessary, especially if it is a male dog and the driving force is a bitch in season. But it does not defend the whole area it has learnt to know—in this respect, the word territory is misleading. It is more a question of hunting-grounds rather than territory. In a hunting mood, a dog may sometimes find itself outside the area it knows, and the mood a dog is in when hunting is perhaps the reason why after hunting it may find it difficult to find its way home. There is no real evidence that dogs possess the ability to find their way home over a longer distance.

In this connection a dog's ability to expect definite events at exactly the time they usually occur should be mentioned. A dog has a clear *concept of time,* a kind of internal clock, which is more or less as accurate as a human's. Every dog-owner knows that a dog usually waits for its master to come home at the time he usually does and that a dog expects food at definite times, etc. My dachshunds usually invite my wife to make the afternoon coffee two hours after dinner, even if the dachshunds happen to be so full at the time that they are not even interested in possible titbits, and sleep calmly through the actual coffee-drinking. Unfortunately no research has been done to show how exact a dog's 'internal clock' is. But it should also be remembered that a dog's ability to expect the right event at the expected time may also depend on associations with our own behaviour, or to occurrences which we ourselves cannot prove, or which we happen not to have noticed.

MOODS

Apart from those moods directly associated with instinctive activity and which in some ways constitute a part of those activities, a dog has moods with no associations with the instinctive activity apparatus. To a certain extent, fear when a dog has 'a bad conscience' is one of these. But this is very close to real direct fear, with its flight reactions and demonstrations of subordinance. On the other hand, the type of emotions which from a human point of view would be called jealousy, disappointment, grief, joy and love are quite different. No one who knows a dog can avoid noticing that it has some kind of emotional life. It is also quite obvious that these moods have the same background as the equivalent moods in ourselves and sometimes also have the same consequences.

Jealousy or envy is extremely common in cases when dogs of a not very social breed grow up in the same home and are cared for by the same people. My dachshunds are an excellent example of this. In certain situations, they are markedly jealous of each other, and if anyone shows one of them a special favour, for several hours this sometimes influences the other's behaviour towards the one who outshone it to the other's disadvantage. An example would illuminate these reactions. If I take just the older dachshund on a trip to our summer place, the younger one left behind does not make importunate demands to persuade me to take her too. But when I return home later, the younger dachshund, the daughter, is not only angry with her mother but also quite often very disinclined to welcome me home with her customary exuberance. Her anger towards her mother passes in a few minutes, but her distrust towards me, who has so crudely betrayed her hopes, has several times lasted for hours. Sometimes I have even been able to see traces of it the next morning. Finally she overcomes her bad temper, usually quite suddenly, and comes at my bidding, at which she shows great joy. What purpose has this jealousy, this bad temper towards the person whom the dog expects to take her on a highly desirable outing, but who dashes the dog's hopes? Presumably similar situations in principle arise in litters of pups and wolf-cubs. An individual which is usually friendly or usually leads the others, brutally rejects every attempt to play or go off on a hunting expedition, etc. The mood this individual's behaviour causes in other members of the pack leads to a swift breaking up of the pack, swift release from dependency. This is undoubtedly a biologically significant process.

A mood of grief occurs quite often among dogs, not only when a person has gone away or has vanished from the dog's environment in general, but also when a good dog-friend has vanished. This mood is characterised by pronounced inactivity. The same situation may also release at least indications to searching reactions and sometimes the reaction of howling. The dog visits the places where the person or the other dog was usually to be found. There are no real general rules on how a dog reacts to the death of another dog, but in many cases death has been a result of illness, and the sick dog has kept away or has not been active. In addition, some sick dogs obviously have a smell which makes healthy dogs avoid them, or simply be afraid when they smell the scent. I have seen this many times. Whelping bitches may whine for a while when a pup dies at birth, then lick the dead pup and also defend it. A Dobermann buried her dead pup. If all pups are taken away when small, most bitches show great anxiety and different kinds of searching behaviour for varying lengths of time.

In its relation to other dogs, a dog does not show any definite sexual love, but an involvement bound to the bitch's season, which in the male is pronounced even when the bitch is not nearby. This mood is expressed in anxiety, a very much increased inclination to beg for walks (to the beloved's territory, of course!), decreased appetite and increased inclination to aggression, which in some cases is also directed towards people. These symptoms are also found in some bitches, but not so markedly. These symptoms of love, which can be found with various modifications in many mammals, naturally have the function of increasing the opportunities for the two partners meeting. They perhaps also emphasise the choice made, by the greater rivalry which arises through the favours of the opposite sex. In non-sexual relations to other dogs, a dog may be dominated by a large number of moods. Often the dog is good friends with a number of dogs which it has gradually got to know especially well. They are playmates, for instance, or hunting companions, or dogs it just greets in a friendly way. But dogs also often have special enemies, to which all relations are dominated by aggression.

DOGS IN A HUMAN ENVIRONMENT

The ability to interpret human moods

Every dog in a good home devotes a great deal of time to following its owners' activities. During its life with the members of the family, it learns not only to react to their actions, words, deeds, etc., but even to anticipate when they may be expected to do what the dog is interested in. A dog quickly learns to associate direct actions and words with useful advantages to itself; the serving of food, preparations for walks or for outings of other kinds. But associations in many cases go so much further into such subtle details in human behaviour that they are difficult to describe. A dog can evidently react even to things caused by brain activity which has not yet come into our consciousness, but which influences our movements.

My male Scottish terrier has given me an excellent example of a dog's capacity to 'anticipate' its master's behaviour before he himself is aware of what he is going to do. The situation was as follows: the Scottie came with me on a long motor-boat trip to count birds among the outer skerries. The boat was equipped with an inboard engine and the Scottie use to lie on the pleasantly warm engine cover as soon as the engine was definitely running. But it was afraid of the banging noise of the cylinders when starting up, and expressed this in loud barking and an inclination to rush at the engine whenever it heard this noise. It barked at our departure from every skerry. But after a few times it learnt that our return in the direction of the motor-boat meant that the engine would start up that hateful noise. So it began to bark beforehand. This went so far that it began to bark and retreat towards the motor-boat as soon as it discovered the slightest hesitation in my movements during the nest-counting, which occurred while walking in the direction away from the boat towards the farthest point of the skerry. Finally, it noted my hesitation beforehand, in fact before I myself was clearly conscious of the fact that there was no point in going on any further. Naturally this strong effective attitude to the engine's starting noise made this reaction to subtleties in its master's movements much easier. The dog was tensely expectant: 'When will he turn back? That engine is so incredibly annoying and unpleasant.' This experience shows the dog's sharp ability to observe, which in its turn is the explanation why many lay people may have the impression that a dog can read a person's thoughts. The fact is that a dog in some cases can notice the slightest change in its master's behaviour as well as changes of which he himself is not aware.

A dog takes certain features in a person's face in a way which tallies fairly well with the way in which a dog sees equivalent features in another dog's face. If you grimace and show your teeth and the dog has no experience of this joke, it becomes anxious, afraid or slightly aggressive. Naturally this is an innate reaction, adapted from dogs' frequent baring of teeth. Dogs see quite well from each other's expressions and head movements where the stimulus is that releases the interest. The position of the ears and direction of the nose seem to play a much more important rôle than the direction of the eyes. In accordance with this, it is probably almost impossible to get a dog to see something which one stares at but does not point out in any way, even if that something may be expected to interest the dog very much. If one of two dogs takes up an alert-position the other quickly directs its nose in approximately the same direction and then usually sees the object of interest very quickly. Neither has a dog the ability to understand a person's pointing without previous self-training, but it learns quite quickly to see or look for objects at least approximately in the direction one points out with a gesture. Dogs also quickly learn to look wherever one is thinking of throwing a ball.

It is very rare that my dachshunds bark each in a different direction in a situation in which only one of them, the one that began, has seen or heard whatever caused the barking. Not until the other one discovers nothing in the 'pointed-out' direction does she also begin to look for the cause in other directions. Perhaps she then discovers something else to bark at, or something which, now activated, she barks at, but which she would otherwise ignore. Dogs can in fact, unintentionally of course, 'lure' each other on to bark at things which are actually quite harmless. The mood of barking at something dangerous can be transferred very easily, if the one's bark is a sign to the other that there is something dangerous nearby, even if there is not. With good opportunities for control, however, this mood ebbs quickly away if nothing worrying can be found. But with less good opportunities, in the dark, for instance, the anxiety remains much longer.

Our own ability to interpret changes in a dog's mood can easily be trained so that it may even surpass the dog's. It often happens that a dog does not react clearly to very small changes in another dog's mood. Very small changes of mood are not in fact necessarily of social significance. When it comes to interpreting her mother's oscillation between play-mood and aggression, my younger dachshund bitch is just as skilful as the members of the family, but not more skilful. Many quite unnecessary conflicts between a dog and people the dog does not know would be avoided if people in general would take a little more notice of a dog's facial expression and bother to interpret it. Better results would also be reached with the mild training one should give every domestic dog. Many a mother allows her child to pat a strange dog, irrespective of whether this strange dog is showing signs of aggression or bad temper, or perhaps has already been doing so before the child appeared. It is not to be wondered at that situations like this sometimes lead to accidents. A good rule is: Don't pat strange dogs. But if one must do so, one should take note of the dog's expression—or rather its mood as shown by its posture, movements and facial expression. If these betray that the dog is in a bad temper, then one has only oneself to blame, although the law says that a dog-owner is responsible for a dog not being a danger to its surroundings. A normal domestic or sporting dog is, however, no danger to strange people so long as no one directly provokes the dog to aggression. This may also happen through misdirected friendliness.

'Sense of humour'

It can be said with good grounds that a dog has a kind of sense of humour. In certain situations anyhow a dog's reactions certainly have the same background as our own reactions to what we regard as humorous. If there is suddenly an obvious contradiction between impressions which the sense of smell and hearing give of something the dog knows very well, and the object's appearance, then the dog reacts with facial expressions, movements and sounds of a very varied kind. But naturally the object must not be so frightening that the dog becomes definitively afraid. Reactions of this kind appear very clearly if the dog sees some member of the family disguised in some way, especially if the face is hidden or changed. Two of my three Scottish terriers found obvious delight in being confronted with disguised members of the family, who again and again appeared in different outfits. Changes in these friends' appearance often released a series of joyful vocalisations, the dogs at first having behaved expectantly but hesitantly. Some movements in situations such as these are typical anticipatory actions. Greater alterations in a person's face are not necessary for a dog to react. A pair of glasses, or a different pair of glasses from usual, a scarf over your head, or a wig, are each enough in combination with some non-typical clothes on the person in question for a dog to be in the mood to play this game of disguise.

In some cases, however, a dog shows surprisingly little interest

K

in the appearance of clothes, while clothing in another situation is decisive for a dog's behaviour. People change their clothes so often that at home a dog does not regard clothing as characteristic of a member of the family, so long as the clothes do not make an impression too far from the norm. But at a distance characteristic clothing may add strongly to the dog's recognition of a member of the family. A dog would behave quite normally even if one suddenly took it out for a walk when one was dressed in only a nightdress. But even clearer is a dog's reaction when we take out clothes we usually wear for trips to our summer place, for instance, or hunting clothes. A dog associates certain clothes with trips to places where great pleasure awaits them, and the dog then may give free rein to pleasure-denoting instinctive actions.

Some dogs like playing hide-and-seek just for the sake of the game, in other words without receiving any other reward than that, after tense expectation, they find the person who has hidden himself and whom they know well. This game also has a certain touch of humour. The more unexpected the hiding-place is, the more joyful and excited the dog becomes when it finds the hider. Just the sight of a person well known to a dog in a very surprising place can make the dog carry out anticipatory actions released by a joy-dominated mood.

The ability to understand pictures, etc.

Many dogs show clear reactions to pictures, but only if these are so big that they reflect some object significant to the dog in a fairly natural field of vision at a slightly greater distance. Small pictures close to do not arouse a dog's interest. Some dogs find obvious pleasure in seeing pictures projected on to a wall or a screen, and others react only to the first picture, investigate it, perhaps try to walk behind the screen, and when they find nothing, lose interest in the pictures. Silent films may arouse interest for a brief spell. Animal films with sound on television may arouse sufficient interest that for several minutes at a time a dog follows everything that is happening on the film very carefully. However, dogs do not usually react by barking when, for instance, a dog barks in a film. Not even typical prey-animals or their vocalisations arouse enough impulse to activity, only interest. It does happen that dogs walk up to the television screen and also that they try to see what is behind the set, but although they find nothing of interest, interest in the programme inside the set remains with undiminished strength. It can perhaps be said that a dog knows that it is not reality, but like humans, it reacts to what is being shown, especially if it is what in reality would release hunting or aggressive activity. But a dog is not usually able to concentrate on television for more than a few minutes at a time. Then it suddenly falls asleep, probably a kind of anticipatory reaction. If the dog sees or hears a member of the family on television, it reacts only for a second, just long enough for there to be time to see that it has realised that the picture looks like a person it knows.

I have once or twice tried to tell my dachshunds things on the telephone with words like 'trip to the country', 'meat', or something else which in direct speech would arouse the most violent joy, even if the dog cannot see who is speaking. But on the telephone a voice is evidently so distorted that a dog remains uncertain about both what is being said and who is saying it. A certain interest has been traced, but not the violent reaction the dog would otherwise immediately show. Dogs generally react to words known to them, even if it is a strange person speaking them.

Dogs can relatively easily associate the ringing of the telephone with someone going up to the telephone to answer it. If the telephone goes on ringing, i.e. if no one answers it, a dog easily gets worried. Presumably it is unpleasant for a dog to hear the telephone repeating its sharp signal over and over again, and answering it entails that this unpleasantness will stop. A normal invitation action ('come on') may be released if no one replies. The dog goes up to a person and nudges him or her with its nose. In this way a dog can without training manage the unlikely and useful action of intervening and asking people to answer the telephone.

Why do we like our dogs?

The answers to this question vary according to the reasons why we have acquired a dog. Some people keep a dog just for company, others just for sport, some just so that the dog can be used for breeding and making money for the owner, others perhaps get a dog for reasons of fashion or vanity, and finally some people maintain they keep a dog primarily in order to study dog behaviour. Most people who get a dog and take it home while it is still a pup soon find that with the best will in the world they cannot avoid emotional involvement with it. And the person who can see nothing else in a pup except a very troublesome and annoying creature, which to crown everything often chews things up, from nylon stockings to expensive upholstery, rugs and books, should not be a dog-owner, at least so long as he or she lives in a city flat, and preferably not otherwise either. Both the dog and its owner will suffer. A dog is once and for all not just an object in the home, but a living creature, which is able to live its life fully in the highly artificial environment our home offers it and with the social relations we can give it.

At the same time, a dog still retains most of its forefathers' natural reactions both to its own species and to the most varying situations in a natural environment. The helplessness of a pup is the first thing which appeals to our innate reactions. It is snub-nosed and chubby, and so we think it is sweet. It moves cautiously, wobbling and uncertain. So we find it rather touching, if we dare admit to such an emotion. The pup successfully appeals to human tending behaviour, although it by no means resembles a human child. When the pup then develops, its development arouses our interest. We can hardly help being influenced by the trust the pup begins to show in us, presuming we handle it correctly. When we shortly no longer have a pup but a young dog in our home, the dog has already such a firm position in our emotional world that its changed appearance does not lessen our unreflecting delight in keeping a dog. It becomes part of our own home environment and we await its joyful greetings when we go home, and it is also often a good and useful companion. A dog can be troublesome in many ways; it forces us to make arrangements on journeys, it makes us take healthy exercise and entails the expense of its food and licence. And in spite of all this, people keep dogs!

And when the dog eventually, all too soon, grows old, we should remember that no wild animal of the lupus type would be able to survive with its sight, hearing and the vital functions of its internal organs strongly diminished by age. Marked symptoms of old age in a dog mean that we have already given the dog a few years' extra life. It is natural that a dog should be allowed to die without pain when it can no longer live a normal life, even in the peaceful environment we give it. When we perhaps hesitate to intervene, it is in the long run mostly because we are afraid of the grief a dog's death may cause us. And when the old dog has gone, it is natural to get another one, a pup, which probably seems to us strangely stupid, but which nevertheless within a few days wins our affection and which with friendliness, consistency and a scrap of ethological knowledge, we can shape into a faithful but at the same time personable, individual dog.

BIBLIOGRAPHY

Below are listed a number of important investigations into wolf- and dog-behaviour, a few works which outline some dog-behaviour, and a few general ethological works which make a good introduction to modern ethological research.

Borg, Marelius & Skårman, S. *Heredity, breeding and diseases.* (Dog Training and Dog Care 2.) LT's förlag, Stockholm, 1962.

Dethier, V. & Stellar, E. *Animal Behavior.* Prentice Hall, New York.

Dog Training and Dog Care I–II. 2nd Edition. LT's förlag, Stockholm 1967. (Authors: Pehrsson, Bergman, Nordström, Borg, Marelius, Matson, Skårman, Swedrup.)

Fabricius, E. *Ethology.* Svenska bokförlaget, Stockholm, 1961.

Fischel, W. *Die Seele des Hundes.* Paul Parey. Berlin-Hamburg, 1961.

v. Frish, O. *Vier Hunde und ihr Herr.* Kosmos Verlag, 1965.

Fuller, J. L., 'Individual Difference in the Activity of Dogs'. *Journal of Comparative and Phys. Psychology*, 41: 339–347. 1946.

Grzimek, B. 'Weitere Vergleichsversuche mit Wolf und Hund'. *Zeitschrift für Tierpsychologie*, 5: 59–73. 1942. 'Tötung von Menschen durch befreundete Hunde II'. *Zeitschrift für Tierpsychologie*, 11: 147–149. 1954.

Heimburger, N. 'Das Markierungsverhalten einiger Caniden'. *Zeitschrift für Tierpsychologie*, 16: 104–113. 1959.

Koehler, O. 'Von unbenannten Denken'. *Verhandlungen der Deutschen Zoologischen Gesellschaft*, 202–211. 1953. 'Psychologie des Hundes'. *Kynologischer Weltkongress 1956*, Westfaledruck, Dortmund, 1956.

Kramer, G. 'Beobachtungen an einem von uns aufgezogenem Wolf'. *Zeitschrift für Tierpsychologie*, 18: 91–109. 1961.

Lorenz, K. *Man Meets Dog*, Methuen, London, 1954; *On Aggression*, Methuen, London, 1966.

Ludwig, J. 'Beobachtungen über das Spiel bei Boxern'. *Zeitschrift für Tierpsychologie*, 22: 813–838. 1965.

Menzel, R. & R. 'Welpe und Umwelt'. *Hundeforschung. Neue Folge*, 3: 1–65. 1937.

Meyer-Holzapfel, M. 'Das Spiel bei Säugetieren'. *Handbuch der Zoologie*, 8: 2, Liefereung 10: 1–36. 1956.

Mowat, F. *Don't cry wolf*. Stockholm, 1967.

Murie, A. 'The Wolves of Mount McKinley'. *Fauna of the National Parks of United States*, Fauna Series 5. Washington, 1944.

Rosengren, A. 'A Study of Colour Discrimination in Dogs'. *Acta Zoologica*, Fennica 121, 20 pp. 1968.

Schenkel, R. 'Ausdrucks-Studien an Wölfen'. *Behaviour*, 1: 81–129. 1947.

Schönberger, D. 'Beobachtungen zum Fortplanzungsbiologie des Wolfes, Canis Lupus'. *Zeitschrift für Säugetierkunde*, 31: 171–178. 1965.

Scott, J. P. 'The Social Behaviour of Dogs and Wolves: An Illustration of Sociabiological Systematics'. *Annals of the New York Academy of Sciences* 51: 1009–1021. 1950.

Scott, J. P. *Animal Behavior*. University of Chicago Press. Natur och Kultus, 1962.

Scott, J. P. & Fuller, J. L. *Genetics and the Social Behavior of the Dog*. 468 pp. Chicago Press, 1965.

Seitz, A. 'Untersuchungen über angeborene Verhaltenweisen bei Caniden'. *Zeitschrift für Tierpsychologie*, 4: 1–46; 12: 436–489; 16: 717–771. 1950, 1955, 1959.

Swedish Dog Dictionary. Ica-förlaget, Västerås, 1966.

Tembrock, G. *Verhaltensforschung*. Gustav Fischer, Jena, 1961.

INDEX